The Coach Horse

Also by Stanley M. Jepsen

Trees and Forests
The Gentle Giants

The Coach Horse
Servant with Style

Stanley M. Jepsen

South Brunswick and New York: A. S. Barnes and Company
London: Thomas Yoseloff Ltd

A. S. Barnes and Co., Inc.
Cranbury, New Jersey 08512

Thomas Yoseloff Ltd
Magdalen House
136-148 Tooley Street
London SE1 2TT, England

Library of Congress Cataloging in Publication Data

Jepsen, Stanley M
The coach horse.

Includes bibliographical references and index.
1. Coach horses. I. Title.
SF312.J46   636.1'4   75-20612
ISBN 0-498-01789-3

Jacket photograph of Mr. John Richards of Macclesfield, Cheshire, England, driving his team of middle weight Irish Hunters to the Sheffield Telegraph Road Coach—winners of the North Challenge Trophy, Northern Driving Championship Driving Show, 1973.

PRINTED IN THE UNITED STATES OF AMERICA

To my wife,
Ruth,
and our children,
who have joyfully shared my love of horses

Contents

Acknowledgments

The author wishes to express his gratitude for all the courtesy, encouragement, help, and advice given him in the preparation of this book by the following: Mr. Paul E. Bolton, Executive Secretary, American Hackney Horse Society, Peekskill, N.Y.; The Royal Danish Embassy, Washington, D.C.; Deutsche Reiterliche Vereinigung (FN), Warendorf, Germany; Mr. Paul H. Downing, Editor Emeritus, The Carriage Journal, Staten Island, N.Y.; Mr. A. C. Drowne, Administrative Vice President and Secretary, American Morgan Horse Association, Inc., Hamilton, N.Y.; Mr. F. W. Eustis, sculptor, Cincinnati, Ohio; Mr. J. Cecil Ferguson, Providence, R.I.; German Equestrian Federation, Hanover, Germany; The Embassy of the Federal Republic of Germany, Washington, D.C.; Mr. Philip B. Hofmann, New Brunswick, N.J.; Interstate Printers & Publishers, Inc., Danville, Ill.; my son, Jeffrey S. Jepsen (photos as indicated); Mr. J. W. Lane, Jr., Vienna, Va.; Lt. Col. Sir John M. Miller, CVO, DSO, MC, KBE., Crown Equerry, The Royal Mews, Buckingham Palace, London, England; The Royal Netherlands Embassy, Washington, D.C.; Mr. Jesse Ostroff, National Agricultural Library; Mr. Melvin M. Peavey, Editor/Publisher, Horse World, Lexington, Ky.; Pitkin Pictorials Ltd., London, England; Mr. John Richards, Horse Drawn Carriages, Ltd., Macclesfield, Cheshire, England; Mr. and Mrs. Thomas Ryder, Seabrook Farm, Salem, N.J.; Mr. John M. Seabrook, Philadelphia, Pa.; Mr. Chauncey Stillman, New York City; The Royal Swedish Embassy, Washington, D.C.; Frederick Warne & Co., Ltd.; London, England; and Mr. Philip Weber, Cleveland, Ohio; The Westmorland Davis Memorial Foundation, Inc., Morven Park, Leesburg, Va.

Introduction

Before he emigrated to the United States, my maternal grandfather was a coachman on a count's estate in East Prussia, Germany. I never knew him, as he was killed working on the railroad in West Virginia when my mother was only six. So, any love of horses or knowledge of coaching he imparted to me came by a most imperceptible route, despite his reported great degree of these attributes.

My love of horses received it greatest cultivation during my boyhood, which was spent on a farm in Delaware County, Ohio. This was during the time when the use of houses for agricultural purposes reached its apex in the United States. The period also marked the close of the "horse and buggy" days. My interest level reached its apogee with the acquisition of my own three-gaited saddle horse, a level from which it has never returned.

Whatever its derivation, my fondness for horses has been tempered in recent years with a concern for the scarcity of horses in the American scene. The decline in numbers of all kinds of horses became so noticeable by the 1960s, that horse fanciers expressed concern that certain breeds might become extinct. Happily, for horses in general such a tragedy has been averted. The always popular light horses began to enjoy an upsurge in numbers about the end of the 1950s. From approximately 3 million horses in the country in 1960, their numbers have increased to an estimated 10 million. The great majority of these are light horses and ponies, used largely for pleasure. However, the heavy draft horses are also making a dramatic comeback. Many state fairs are expanding their draft horse exhibits, and county fairs are either reinstating their draft horse shows or starting them because of popular demand. Pulling contests have developed an unprecedented following the country over.

Author at the reins (left) of a team of Oldenburg horses from Germany, imported by Mr. John Seabrook of Seabrook Farm, Salem, New Jersey. On the driver's seat with him is Tom Ryder, leading authority on formal driving and author of the driving manual, On the Box Seat. *The vehicle is a Beaufort phaeton. (Photo by the author's son, Jeffrey S. Jepsen.*

But what of the "in between" breeds? What has been the fate of the horses between the light breeds and the heavy drafters? The horses bred to work — bred for versatility, that could be unharnessed and ridden at a fast and comfortable gait. Horses that were not too big to be a child's mount nor too proud to pull a plow, serving the farmer as faithfully as captains and kings. Horses epitomized by the coach horse, those gallant dependables who always served with style.

By definition, a coach horse is a horse used or adapted for drawing a coach. This is indeed a broad definition, but, the coach horse's great versatility, as well as variation, was brought about by the great variety of vehicles he was expected to draw, and the conditions under which he was expected to draw them. Difficulty of definition is emphasized when one considers it was the horses of this category that thundered by with the smoking and flashing steam pumper of the glorious days of the horse-drawn fire engines. It was the same horses that wheeled the caissons and artillery into position in both World War I and early World War II. These horses also in World War I, carried Kaiser Wilhelm's crack Uhlans on their dreaded cavalry raids. This same type of horse served on the picturesque stagecoaches of our own country's expanding

A team of Holstein horses, another famous German breed of coach horses, hitched in tandem. Note that the lead horse has a breast collar while the wheel horse has a neck collar.

The "Tally-Ho!" road coach driven by Mr. Phillip B. Hofmann with his team of Holsteiners.

period. These horses still draw the coaches of state in many foreign lands, and carry the bodies of our own national heroes to their final resting place, adding the last touch of dignity and honor that can be shown in the homage of a grateful people.

We can arbitrarily separate horses (14.2 hands or over) from ponies (up to 14.2 hands) on the basis of height at the withers. Or, on the basis of weight, we can separate light horses (up to 1,400 pounds) from draft horses (1,400 pounds and over). But where does the coach horse fit in this category? At the risk of rousing a long dormant controversy, I will say the coach horse falls in the bracket 1,100 pounds to 1,500 pounds.

One of my horseman friends responded immediately to this statement with, "Why, the finest coach-and-four I ever saw didn't have a horse in it that weighed over 1,000 pounds, and all four were perfectly matched!" Of course! Many of us have seen teams of diminutive ponies pulling miniature coaches in parades, at fairs, and at other gala occasions.

By way of contrast, one evening not long ago I drove my family into Howard and Mary Streaker's Clearview Farm, West Friendship, Maryland, just as they were about to hitch up two of their marvelous Shires in tandem to a beautifully restored vis-a-vis. Each of these Shires weighs at least a ton. Yet, their beauty and grace, with their dark coats reflecting the flickerings of the oil coach lamps, made the most pleasant

Mr. Douglas Nicholson of Durham, England, with his private drag at the Windsor Show. The horses are Gelderland horses—among the finest coach horse breeds from the Netherlands.

14

Mr. Douglas Nicholson driving his four-in-hand of Gelderland horses through Windsor Great Park during the 1966 Royal Ascot.

Mr. Phillip Hofmann driving his Holsteiners in the Liberty Run Drive at the 1973 Philadelphia Horse Show.

impression on all. As we followed them out the driveway, someone remarked this indeed was going in style.

All of which substantiates my original statement regarding the difficulty of defining the coach horse precisely. Neither the ponies nor the drafters should be included with the coach horses. Certainly they can, and do, draw coaches and carriages beautifully, but certain horses have been bred for this purpose — superb horses — and they are the ones we are going to take a closer look at in this book.

An additional introductory statement seems appropriate at this point. Why are people beginning to be concerned about so many things that were important in yesterday's way of life? I believe it is more than nostalgia. Nostalgia in itself accomplishes nothing, but it can be an important factor in motivating great efforts of restoration. It can help persons realize that some of the finer things of yesterday are very important in a well-balanced, healthful, and inspired life today.

Several generations have been denied the opportunities to become acquainted with coach horses and coaching. (Even more generations have lived since such sights were commonplace?) Perhaps this is one reason why dedicated persons, both here and abroad, continue active in the breeding and training of coach horses — to let the world again see beauty in action, grace in motion, and distinction in service. I suspect though the main reason is still the love of these magnificent animals.

The Coach Horse

1
Coach Horses in General

It is a little known fact that man first used the horse by driving him rather than by riding him. It requires only a little imagination to picture those ancients who had to capture the horse if he was to be used for anything other than food. To do this required getting a rope of some kind, or a thong, and fastening this on the horse. Once this was accomplished the horse could be tied up. Unless he was tied to an immovable object, it was soon learned that the horse could drag a considerable weight. If the object which he was fastened to happened to be a log, and the log was not too heavy, man could stand or sit on it, and be pulled along also.

Man's ingenuity soon fashioned a crude sled, which, along with the addition of wheels, became a crude chariot, without springs. How long the horse was used to draw only such vehicles we do not know. As for riding on the animal, that took a lot of time and courage. In due course, however, the men who were driving and caring for the horse found they could manage him while on his back. This was done without the modern inventions of a saddle or bridle. In the earliest sculptures we see the horse depicted as ridden bareback and without bridle. There is also abundant written testimony in support of this mode of equitation being practiced by the early Greeks. It is also an ascertained fact that when the Romans invaded Great Britain they found the people in possession

A shooting brake.

Nice action on a hunter-type gig.

A park drag in 1905.

of horses, and using them for their chariots as well as for the purposes of riding.

It was the ingenious Greeks, however, who invented the snaffle-bridle, and both rode and drove with its aid. This was after the establishment of the Olympian games, in which chariot races formed an essential feature.*

The curb-bit was invented by the Romans, or, at least, was first used by them. Both the Romans and the Greeks were ignorant of the use of the stirrup, and either vaulted on their horses, used a short ladder, or used the back of a slave as a stepping stone.

The earliest proven period that the stirrup was in use was in the time of the Norman invasion of England. The incidents of this event in history were recorded on the Bayeux tapestry by the wife of William the Conqueror. This tapestry depicted the stirrup as a part of the trappings of the horse. Shoeing was not practiced by either the Greeks or the Romans, and only in cases of lameness was the foot protected by a sandal, which, however, was sometimes tipped with iron.

Until some time after the beginning of the Olympian Games, the use of the horse was limited to war and the chase. These games were held every four years, and are supposed to have started about 774 B.C. As it was not until the 23rd Olympiad that the horse was introduced in the arena, the birth of horse-racing may be fixed at about the year 680 B.C. At first the horses were ridden, and the distance was about four miles. In the 25th Olympiad the chariot was introduced, and after this time

*Adapted in part from: John Henry Walsh, *The Horse and the Stable and the Field*, 1880.

21

became the prevailing instrument of testing the speed and powers of the Grecian horse. Here, also, the distance was about four miles, but as a pillar was to be rounded several times, the race depended quite as much on the skill of the charioteer as on the qualities of the horses.

During the Dark Ages, we have no reliable history to guide us concerning the development of the horse. From the time Vegetius wrote on the veterinary art in the fourth century we are left to grope in the dark until the time of the Stuarts in England, when attention was first directed toward improving the various breeds of horses.

It is not my intention to give a history of the horse. This has been done many times by scholars. For a brief history of the horse one may refer to the first chapter of this author's book on draft horses, "The Gentle Giants", (Arco Publishing Co. 1971). Many other volumes have been written on the subject, which precludes my devoting much space to the history of the horse in general. I will, however, assign adequate space to the subject in the treatment of the respective breeds.

It should suffice at this stage to point out that with the passage of time great variations developed between the many different breeds of horses. This necessitated the division of horses into different classes, which is really based on the kind of work each class is expected to do. The various purposes for which horses are employed demand animals especially adapted to their respective assignments. Those persons who

Lippizaner mares being trained for driving at Piber, Austria.

The winning coach, a private coach entered by W.A. Gilbey, Ltd., in the Coaching Championship, The International Horse Show at White City, London, 1956.

have made a study of the subject know that heavy coaches or carriages require large, powerful horses, which in a smaller or lighter vehicle would produce the effect of "a man doing a boy's work".* Therefore, it may be said that the division of horses into classes is the result of an endeavor to establish a balance of proportion between the horse and his work. With this in view, various types of horses have been bred with thegreatest of care and attention to the development of those qualifications which make them particularly adaptable; the combination of strength, symmetry, disposition, and manners, for some specific work. The result is that the well bred horse of today represents one of the several distinct types (the coach horse, for instance), having an inherent aptitude for performing a limited range of work.

The purchaser of a horse first needs to consider for what purpose he needs a horse. Is the animal to be used for heavy draft, as a coach or carriage horse, a light harness horse, an agricultural horse, or a saddle horse? All of these have different points of excellence and distince

*Adapted in part from: James A. Garland, *The Private Stable* (Little, Brown & Co., 1903)

23

A Sunday afternoon in Lincoln Park, Duluth, Minn., 1910.

qualifcations.* The heavy draft horse and agricultural horse are the least difficult to select; the coach or carriage horse next; then the light harness horse, and lastly, the saddle horse, which is the most difficult of all to find near perfection. The heavy draft horse requires only great power and weight, with a fast walking action, or moderate trot. The agricultural horse requires strength, quickness, activity, hardihood, and courage. The coach or carriage horses are to be estimated very differently; size, fine figure, great show, stylish action, and moderate speed are all needed.

The best coach or carriage horses are of two general types: First, is the small, compact, quick stepping animals, ranging in height between 14.2 and 15.2 hands. When well bred and carefully selected they combine strength with great activity and hardiness, and are consequently excellent for all around use. Second, is the larger class of coach horse, resembling the hunter in conformation. Many of the best of these horses are in fact hunter bred and consequently have some thoroughbred blood in their veins.

*Adapted in part from James A. Garland, *The Private Stable* (Little, Brown, & Co., 1903)

By crossing the thoroughbred horse with the trotting bred horse, or the trotter with the Hackney or French coach, a variety of types has been produced. Such cross breds have supplied the demands of buyers more successfully than most pure breds.

The large family coach horse, with flowing mane and tail, is always popular with owners of large carriages. When driven as a pair they produce a fine effect and are very useful for heavy work. They should be strong, but of quick, light action.

Since we are talking about the different types of coach horses being bred for the different kinds of work they are expected to do, it follows that this is an admirable place to discuss briefly the various types of vehicles these horses draw. Volumes have been written on the subject of coaches and carriages alone. Therefore, this insertion is intended merely to help the reader, along with the pictures incorporated in this book, to visualize a few of the vehicles and the types of horses best suited for each.

The Coach — All panelled carriages with seats for four persons inside, and an elevated coachman's seat, are designated coaches. They are generally thought of as being closed, and having a hard top.*

The Caleche — This vehicle is of French origin. It is a carriage with a leather top, and portable glass shutters on the sides, and a panelled front with a sliding window. The whole front may be removed in a few minutes, making it an elegant Barouche. It may be said this was the original convertible.

The Landau — The Landau is similar to the Caleche, without the portable front and the glass sides. The entire top is of leather, supported by folding joints at each corner.

The Barouche — The Barouche is made for four persons inside, and has an elevated coachman's seat. It has either a leather half-top over the back seat, or an extension top covering the four seats inside.

The Brougham, or *Coupe* — This vehicle is really a half-coach. The body has room for two persons inside, and an elevated coachman's seat.

The Rockaway — An American invention, the Rockaway has a plain square or straight body, with a standing top and leather curtains. Built for four or six persons, all seats are on the same level. Some Rockaways have panelled sides and glass windows. A distinctive characteristic of all Rockaways is the roof, which always extends over the front or driver's seat.

The Brett — This French vehicle is really a half-top Barouche. One very noticeable characteristic of all Bretts is that all the lines of the body are at right angles. Bretts generally have four seats inside, and an

*Adapted in part from: Henry Wm. Herbert, *Hints to Horse Keepers* (New York: Orange Judd Co., 1888).

Four-in-hand on a Dutch mail coach, Amsterdam, Holland.

elevated coachman's seat.

The Phaeton — This well known vehicle perhaps owes its popularity, especially for summer driving, to its great variety and open airiness. It originally had four seats, with a portable half-top, or without a top. It followed quite naturally that automobiles exhibiting similar styling were also classified as Phaetons.

The work of a single coach horse will, in most cases, be that of drawing a brougham, or its equivalent, weighing from 1,200 to 1,400 pounds approximately. Therefore, a horse measuring from 15.2 hands to 16.1 hands and weighing between, 1,000 and 1,200 pounds is required to draw the carriage, varying according to the size of the vehicle. As some owners wish to use the same horse for a light vehicle in summer, it is advisable to buy a horse somewhat smaller and lighter than would be desirable were the work heavy the year round. It must be born in mind that a large horse is better able to draw a light vehicle than a small animal is to pull a heavy one.

When a horse is being bought for a two-wheeled cart it is of much importance that the animal should have a smooth, even gait. As the shafts hang on a wide strap or "saddle" across the horse's back, they are subject to every up and down motion of the horse. Therefore, unless the horse has a reasonably smooth action the driver may experience

26

Messrs. Rothmans' with their two Irish Hunters, Pell and Mell.

such a rapid jolting motion that it might continue for some time after
the vehicle has stopped.

In buying a pair of horses there are several important considerations
to be thought of after the matter of soundness, etc., have been looked
into. The first requisite is that they should correspond nicely in size and
build. It often happens that a horse measuring the same at the withers

27

Mr. John Richards competing at Eaton Hall, Chester, England, in the new F.E.I. Driving Competitions. This is a team of middle weight Irish Hunters driven to a Stanhope Phaeton. Mr. Richards finished third in the National Championships for Teams in 1973.

A Hungarian carriage.

as his mate will be several inches higher or lower at the quarters. Therefore, it is important that the general outline from the height of the head to that of the quarters of one horse closely corresponds with that of the other. It is one of the rarest and yet most desirable attributes of the pair that they should be of equal muscular and nervous development. Any great dissimilarity is likely to result in one horse being a freer and faster traveler, and he will either tire his slower companion or will exhaust himself drawing more than his share of the weight. A pair working away from the pole, or pressing in, often do so as a result of badly coupled reins. This fault may be corrected by changing their positions, placing the off horse on the near side and vice versa.

If the color of a pair is the same there should be no great difference in its shade, i.e., if one horse is a dark chestnut the other should not be a light chestnut. Roans and bright chestnuts are the hardest of any to match. The darker shades of any color are said, and with some truth, to indicate greater vitality.

The Brougham Horse

The qualifications desirable in a brougham horse were set forth in *The Book of the Horse* by S. Sidney. He said every sort of a horse may be seen hitched to broughams, but the brougham horse proper should have certain qualifications. He should stand well, in a noble attitude,

Tatchanka races at the Moscow Hippodrome.

A Bulgarian horse show being watched by a government delegation in Hungary.

and should move with a certain grandeur of action. He must carry both his head and tail well. In a full-sized brougham, weight is indispensable. In a light, single, or miniature brougham a blood horse is more appropriate. In either case the size of the horse should be in harmony with the size of the carriage. It is as great an error in taste to use a large animal, who may at times almost lift the fore wheels off the ground, as to have a horse so small, and working with his neck so low, that he is lost in the shafts. If full of courage, the latter will very soon be worn out by overweight.

A first-class brougham horse should be long and low, full-barrelled, and from 15 hands to 15.3 hands high, according to the size and weight of the carriage. He should have a broad chest, lofty crest, broad back, flowing mane, and a full tail well carried, presenting a combination of breeding and power. His action should be grand, stately, machine-like, forward action all round. Champing his bit, arching his neck, and bending his knees, he should trot eight miles an hour, and have the ability to do twelve miles an hour.

George A. Weymouth driving his team of American Standard Breds. The photo is •
remarkable in that every horse appears not to be touching the ground.

A Russian Troika with three grey trotters of the Rysaki breed.

31

A parade of light sleighs in Moscow.

A Gelderland horse drawing a small Russian sleigh.

Russian Troika Races at the Moscow Hippodrome.

A double phaeton at the Tbilisi Hippodrome in 1964.

Tatchankas with four horses abreast.

The Victoria Horse

Horses for such a carriage should be similar to those described for a brougham, but as these vehicles are not so heavy, the horse may be correspondingly lighter, quicker stepping, and of a more breedy type. As the horses carry a minimum of harness there is every chance for the display of fine proportion and beauty of outline.

The Phaeton Horse

The very finest horses, of the most brilliant action, look their best attached to a phaeton. The modern phaetons are so much lighter than the old time ones that large horses are quite out of place in them. A phaeton of suitable size may be perfectly well horsed in every respect by horses from 14.3 hands to 15.1 hands. When a pair of horses is used for several purposes, to draw a full-sized brougham or landau, as well as a mail phaeton, 15.2 hands may be found a more useful size. Beyond that height, unless exceedingly well bred, it is difficult to find horses which are pleasant for a gentleman to drive.

The Hansom Horse

Again quoting from S. Sidney, he says, "a high, two-wheeled carriage of this type requires a horse with good trotting action and sound feet. It requires a better horse than a brougham, if not so fashionable, because, in spite of the very best balancing, there must be some weight in going down hills. And he should be fast, equal to 12 or 14 miles per hour when required. Pace and ease of motion are the features of this vehicle."

The Run-about Horse

The horse for this type of vehicle should be between 15 and 15.3 hands. Neither speed nor action need be very pronounced, but they should be combined to a degree that renders the horse a handy one for the purpose for which a carriage of this type is intended.

Droshki harness at the Khrenovsky horse breeding establishment.

The Darebury Phaeton. Prototype of a new F.E.I. Combined Driving Competition vehicle, designed and developed from new by Horse Drawn Carriages Limited, England. The vehicle is fitted with disc brakes, spare wheel, etc., as standard equipment.

The author looking over a Town Coach *of 1851 vintage in the Smithsonian Institute, Washington, D.C. This handsome carriage, the descendant of earlier types such as the coaches of George Washington and many Colonial governors, was a luxury vehicle used by prominent and wealthy persons. Costing $1,225, it was built at the shops of Thomas Goddard of Boston and was originally owned by Amos A. Lawrence, maternal ancestor of Senator Leverett Saltonstall of Massachusetts.*

Landau—*1879. A vehicle of the wealthy, the landau was essentially a coach with a folding top while its lighter relative, the landaulet, was a chariot with a folding top. The carriage shown here was made by Brewster & So., N.Y., for Mrs. Charles Stillman, great grandmother of the donor, Mr. Chauncey Stillman. (Smithsonian Institute, Washington, D.C.)*

The author examining an 1810 Coachee in the Smithsonian Institute, Washington, D.C. This popular vehicle was used in cities as a family carriage. Carrying six passengers, including the driver, it was almost identical to the heavier four seated, 12 passenger stagecoach of the same period. This carriage afforded cover for the driver and in the 1830s became the forerunner of the rockaway. In bad weather the leather side curtains were let down to cover the open sides, and the upper door panel was closed.

The Cabriolet Horse

Although the cabriolet is seldom used at present, it may be of interest to give what was considered a proper type of horse for this vehicle. In shape he was supposed to be nearly faultless, to stand not less than 16 hands, and to have action which could hardly be too extravagant.

The Coach Horse

There is so much difference of opinion as to what is the best and pleasantest style of coach horse to drive that we are not likely to find ourselves in agreement with all our readers upon this subject. Some prefer the big, heavy horse for when that extra power is needed. Others prefer the smaller, compact, and quick-stepping horse, especially since roads are now usually good.

Difference of opinion also exists as to the respective heights of wheelers and lead horses. Some like them exactly the same size. Others prefer a big wheel horse and a smaller leader. Others again like a thick, low wheel horse and a rather tall and slighter leader.

In regard to the stamp of horses for a long and hard day's work, there is nothing that can beat a thoroughbred. The more blood you have in horses you drive, the better you will be able to make long and trying journeys. Still, such animals are scarcely what we should designate by the words "coach horses."

With these preliminary thoughts in mind let us now look at some of the breeds of horses developed specifically for the work involved in drawing coaches. Much of this development was done in the last century, when this mode of transportation was a necessity. Today, the industry is almost entirely for pleasure and for show. This has, however, resulted in the further refinement of the breeds, the elimination of the inferior qualities found in many of the horses in general use a century ago, and a renewed interest in perpetuating this aristocracy of equine society. I am not attempting to list all breeds of coach horses in the world, nor even the finest, but in the following chapters I will attempt to describe and picture some of the leading breeds of coach horses being used today in the western world.

Before beginning the chapters devoted to the respective breeds, however, I would like to relate to the readers a letter I received on March 14, 1974, from Colonel Paul H. Downing, Editor Emeritus of The Carriage Journal, and probably the most knowledgeable person

On the left is a Chaise *(1770) and on the right is a* Gig *(1800). The New England Chaise, a common passenger vehicle of its time is characterized by the cantilever supports, which carry the rear end of the thoroughbraces (leather straps supporting the body and serving as springs). A vehicle of this type without the folding top which is known as a chair, was even more popular than the chaise. The smaller driver's seat shown here is an added feature not often seen. This chaise is also unusual in that it retains the original sectional tires, known as strakes, which were in general use throughout the Colonial period and in some area until the early 19th century. (Smithsonian Institute, Washington, D.C.) Although similar to the New England Chaise, this gig uses C-springs rather than wooden cantilevers to carry the rear ends of the thoroughbraces. Being two-wheeled, it was highly maneuverable; and the large wheels, together with the light construction, made it a relatively comfortable carriage on poor roads. It was popular until the end of the carriage era.*

alive today in the field* of driving, which encompasses the vehicles and the horses themselves:

"As far as I know there has never been any breed of American horse developed for coaching. The French have their coach horses and the Germans theirs, slightly heavier and certainly less smart looking. The coaching horse used in this country was, in nine cases out of ten, animals that were picked up here and there suitable in weight and conformation for the purpose. I do know that the Coaching Club (N.Y.)

*Colonel Paul H. Downing, 77, passed away in June, 1975.

Rockaway–1860. One of the few distinctively American vehicles, the rockaway became one of the most popular family carriages in the late 19th century. Tracing its history to the stage wagon, through the Germantown and the coaches, the earliest version is believed to have originated about 1830 at Jamaica, L.I. Rockaways were built in a variety of styles, characterized by the projecting roof over the driver's seat. The six passenger rockaway shown here resting in a corner of the Smithsonian Museum of History and Technology, is a vehicle of exceptional quality.

Team of Standard Breds drawing a side-seat phaeton at Morven Park, Leesburg, Va.

Single horse drawing a turn-over seat phaeton at Morven Park, Leesburg, Va.

Team of Standard Breds drawing a Rockaway carriage at Morven Park, Leesburg, Va.

41

each spring sent a delegation up to Maine where they selected what they referred to as Maine horses, most of which were said to be "Trotting Bred" but then trotters in those days were of a considerably heavier conformation than those one sees on the track today.

"Probably, the most prominent coaching men of today use Hackneys which are well up to their work and certainly make a very sparkling show. Two other gentlemen use horses imported from Germany which are said to have an admixture of thoroughbred blood. Personally, I find them rather lumbering and lacking in smartness. Another uses a team which are medium weight draft horses and imported from Holland. To my mind, and I repeat my mind, I prefer a team of slightly over 15.2 hands Morgans and of sufficient weight to move any coach ten to twelve miles within the hour. Others are using Hackneys, Percherons, and Crossbreds from Canada.

"The late F. Ambrose Clark owned a number of teams of coaching horses but the last and the ones he said he liked the best were trotters (Standardbreds). When asked why he had selected this breed he said that it was because, 'he wanted to get over the ground' and of course trotters would be most satisfactory in this respect.

"The late Mr. Alfred Vanderbilt, when he took his coach to England, horsed it with 80 American 'Trotting breds' plus of course his famous grey four. But then as I have said, they were horses of considerably more substance than those one finds on the track today.

"The horses I have used personally for four-in-hand driving have just been 'horses' that were up to their work and generally of the same conformation. If I were to horse a four today I would look for 15.2 to 16 hands, half-bred heavy hunters schooled so that they would lift their feet a bit higher than does the average hunter. Certainly in no way that resembles the consuming energy of the Hackneys or the so-called 'show' Morgans. Sizeable and heavy enough American Saddle Horses would also be acceptable providing they were gotten hold of before their extremely high action training and tail breaking.

"This letter may bring forth a number of adverse comments but having been closely associated with horses for the last 60 years, I feel well able to defend my thinking."

Addendum: The following information, which should be of interest to anyone who has read this far into the book, is placed here because it is important coaching history and deserves to be included.

In 1901 there was an organized popular group of young ladies, society debutantes for the most part, interested in coaching and driving. They called themselves *The Ladies' Four-in-Hand Driving Club*, or the LFDC, as it appeared most often in the society page headlines. They copied the men's driving organizations and customs, and added the ladies' touch to attire and imagination to activities. Some became expert horsewomen, and their colorful parades always passed in review of enthusiastic crowds in Central Park.

The LFDC eventually acquired its own coach, which they named "The Arrow," and which the ladies drove on week days to a fashionable inn for lunch, expertly handling either four or six horses. Nor did inclement weather daunt the young fashion plates, for the records show that they held a scheduled club drive of 40 miles in pouring rain.

In view of the new position women have created for themselves in world society, and the affluence of a large segment of that society, should not some women again literally "take the reins" and show the world that several generations of automotive transportation and relative ease of living have not rendered them less capable than the ladies of the LFDC?

2

The Cleveland Bay

This breed of middle-weight horses takes its name from the district of Cleveland in the North Riding of Yorkshire, England, which still remains the chief locale of production. It is an old breed, though some of the claims made for its antiquity probably are exaggerated. That it has a strong infusion of Thoroughbred blood is certain and this has powerfully influenced Cleveland type and character.*

The average Cleveland Bay is about 16 hands high and will weigh from 1,400 to 1,500 pounds. His name signifies his color — a dark, soft, brownish bay, with black points (mane, tail, and lower legs) and solid coat. The presence of white markings, even if inconspicuous, will give rise to doubts of purity of blood.

In appearance this breed suggests a coachy type of grade Thoroughbred, and previous to the advent of motor vehicles, was the favorite English coach horse. He was likewise preferred for many uses in both harness and under saddle, owing to his good disposition, tractability, and easiness to handle. When crossed judiciously with other breeds for the production of all-purpose animals of superior size, (especially hunters and serviceable farm and country types), the Cleveland is of much utility, being a stout and obedient worker, rugged and robust.

The Cleveland Bay has never been extensively imported or bred in

---

*Adapted in part from: Dinsmore and Hervey, *Our Equine Friends*, (Horse and Mule Assn. of America, 1944).

The Cleveland Bay Stallion, Gillshaw Kestrel No. 1952, as a yearling in England. He was foaled in 1970 and imported to the United States as a two year old by Mr. J. W. Lane Jr. of Vienna, Va.

America. However, The Cleveland Bay Society of America, founded in 1885, is maintained at Farnley Farm, White Post, Virginia 22663, with Mr. A. Mackay-Smith as Secretary.

The Cleveland Bay is often claimed to be the only purebred general purpose horse without a trace of Heavy or Cold horse blood. They make first-class heavyweight hunters, and crossed with quality mares the stallions sire excellent jumpers which are often seen in the show ring. Now that both Britain and the United States are undergoing a resurgence of interest in driving, it is to be hoped that the Cleveland Bay will come into his own again as a harness horse. There are many Cleveland Bays among State carriage horses, and when the Queen of England visited York City, England in the summer of 1971 they were chosen as the local breed to draw the carriages taking part in the procession.

It is usually accepted that this breed is a composite one, in other words, that it originally sprang from Eastern sires (Arabs, Barbs, etc.) mated with mares belonging to the districts from whence the breed derives its name. It is the considerable proportion of Thoroughbred blood in the Cleveland Bay, however, which gives the animal its beautiful anatomical configuration.*

Somewhere a little more than a century and a half ago, there were three noted families of Cleveland Bays to name, *The Dart, The Barley Harvest Horse,* and *The Hog Hill Horse.* The Barley Harvest Horse and the Hog Hill Horse are said to have been foaled shortly before the close of the eighteenth century, and it is from these illustrious sires that many of the best Clevelands have descended.

If one were to attempt to trace the geneology of the breed, it would probably go back to the great "war horse," but there is no necessity for this, as the Thoroughbred undoubtedly played a significant part in the composition of the Cleveland Bay. It is stated that there was, about the middle of the eighteenth century, a sire named Old Traveller, traveling in the Yarm district of Yorkshire, and to this Thoroughbred, it is believed, the Cleveland Bay owes its many excellencies.

The breed is modeled on the lines of a coach horse, and when it was established, there is every reason to believe that the aim of the breeders was to produce a class of horse suitable for the work then in existence, i.e. for the coaching purposes, from which it is believed the Yorkshire coach horse was gradually evolved. Now, for a horse to be suitable for

*Adapted in part from: F.T. Barton, *Horses and Practical Horsekeeping* (London: Jarrold and Sons, 1912).

Kestrel being led to the paddock by Mr. Lane, January, 1975.

Kestrel on the lunge rope held by Mr. Lane.

Gillshaw Kestrel, with the author at the halter, at home in Virginia.

47

such heavy vehicular traffic, capable of performing work at what may be termed "top speed," it is perfectly obvious that it must possess courage, endurance, and great strength, which implies that it should be endowed with a maximum amount of bone, muscle, and substance, disposed upon a framework of corresponding strength. The Cleveland Bay deserves to occupy a much more prominent position than it does, though unfortunately, the real merits of this horse have never been as well known as that of certain other varieties.

The conformation of the hind quarters and the carriage of the tail are particularly striking, and certainly characteristic of the breed. The legs and feet are usually "clean," and the joints strong and broad. The Cleveland Bay has not anything like the action of a good Hackney, regard less, it is by no means to be looked down upon as a mover, especially of the fore limbs, in which it can give a good account of both shoulder and knee action. All in all, the Cleveland Bay is a coach horse nonpareil and will always occupy an undisputed niche in the coach horse hall of fame.

Among the great numbers of horses bred in Yorkshire (England) over a long period of time, it is only reasonable to think that there was some differentiation of type according to the work required, and that for riding and pillion a smallish horse on short legs would be in demand. Such horses are still spoken of in Yorkshire as "gallowers." Northeast Yorkshire was, from very early days, famed for its racing "galloways." It is strongly suspected that these were closely related to the original "Cleveland" or "Chapman" horses, the latter name being applied to the favorite horses of the chapmen (travelling salesman) for carrying heavy packs of goods for sale in towns and villages all over England.*

It is interesting to note the very important part North Yorkshire played in the origin and foundation of the racehorse and Thoroughbred as we know them today through the racing "galloways" or "gallowers" of Yorkshire origin. Every Thoroughbred in the world is descended from 78 original mares and three imported Eastern stallions, and of these 78 original mares, over 70 were Yorkshire racing galloways located in North Yorkshire.

Coaches were not known until the reign of Elizabeth I, and the Cleveland type of horse, with its strength, activity, and endurance, was well suited to the first heavy-wheeled vehicles. In due time roads were improved and in·the first quarter of the last century, John Macadam was responsible for such improvement of surface that heavy mail and stage coaches were able to travel from eight to ten miles per hour. The Edinburgh mail was then able to complete its 400 mile journey in 40

*Adapted in part from: J. Fairfax-Blakeborough, *The Cleveland Bay Horse* (The Council of the Cleveland Bay Horse Society).

hours — an average of 10 miles per hour — a hitherto unheard of speed.

There was an immediate demand for horses with speed and endurance to horse the growing number of coaches, and the Cleveland Bay was sold in increasing numbers for this purpose. As the roads improved, nothing could be more natural than that breeders should turn to blood to increase pace, and to patronize sires which had a greater or lesser strain of racing blood in their veins. The blood, which it still holds, unaffected by the modern Thoroughbred, was put into the Cleveland Bay in the days of four-mile racing and of high weights, and to this fact may be ascribed much of its courage and stamina.

Within a few years of the time coaching reached its zenith, steam driven engines and railroads brought coaching to an end. The old family coach of peer and squire was replaced by the barouche, the carriage and pair, the Victoria, and other vehicles. Big prices were paid for high quality, well-matched pairs of 16 or 17 hands. To meet this demand Cleveland Bay mares were mated to large-boned, upstanding Thoroughbreds, and animals descending from such matings, and having perhaps as much as 25 percent of new Thoroughbred blood, came to be called "Yorkshire Coach Horses."

To quote from the late Sir Alfred Pease: "Up to the middle of the last century the Yorkshire Bay Coach Horse (by far the most beautiful breed of coach horse the world has ever seen) was often called the 'New Cleveland Bay' to distinguish it from the 'Old Cleveland Bay,' which was an ancient and distinct breed. The purpose of the Yorkshire Coach Horse has now gone, but the history of its creation is an outstanding example of man's power to produce and to mold to his desire a fixed equine type.

"Throughout the 19th century the demand at home and abroad for Yorkshire Coach Horses for the carriages of the nobility and gentry, and courts of Europe, and of stallions and mares of the breed for the Royal and State studs were enormous. During the height of the London season hundreds of pairs of these magnificent animals might be seen in Hyde Park every afternoon. Until 1884 they were included, by the public at least, in the general term "Cleveland Bays.' They were evolved by taking as a foundation the old, strong Cleveland Bay, which had so long been bred true to type that it could be relied on to transmit its color, style, carriage, flowing lines, level quarters, and free shoulder action to the produce of its cross with the racehorse; the Thoroughbred giving to the Yorkshire Coach Horse that extra quality and faster action that the old Cleveland Bay had not got. About the beginning of the last century coach horse breeders found that the tendency was toward too much blood, and that to preserve the type it was necessary to keep up and recourse to the old Cleveland Bay strains."

The Cleveland Bay Horse Society was formed over 90 years ago. The

Kestrel with the author at the halter, January 26, 1975. Bay with black points (stockings, mane, and tail) is the consistent color of Cleveland Bays.

official pronouncement of the founders of the Society, amongst whose numbers were some of the greatest and most experienced horsemen, horse breeders, and agricultural authorities of that day, was this:

"We assert without fear of contradiction that the old type of Cleveland is the best and most economical animal on the farm; that it will do more work in any given period of time, consume less food, wear less shoe-iron in either slow or fast work on the farm or on the road, than any other breed. Its longevity and lasting qualities are phenomenal. The old type of Cleveland — deep and wide, capable of any kind of farm and road work, fast or slow, should stand about 16 hands high. Back not too long, strong, with muscular loins. Shoulders sloping, deep and muscular. Quarters level, powerful, long and oval, the tail springing well from the quarters. Bone 9 to 10½ inches below the knee."

In the earlier volumes of the Cleveland Bay Stud Book are found recorded instances of the powers of Clevelands as pack horses: (1) Carried 700 pounds 60 miles in 24 hours four times a week. No other animal in the world could do this. Elephants and camels can be found to carry the weight, but how long would they take to do the four journeys. (2) Carried 16 stones (224 lb) 16 miles within the hour — trotting.

The present day importance of the Cleveland Bays may be considered under three headings:

For heavy cultivation on a large, or even on a moderate scale, tractors and heavy equipment are now indispensable, but there are a great many essential jobs on our farms which are carried out as efficiently and with far more economy by horses of the right sort. Among these may be cited short hauls where time is largely taken in loading and unloading (and where the driver often leaves the engine running during the operations), feeding livestock, and many of the operations in haymaking and harvesting. There is no more economic and efficient machine than a power operated grass-mower drawn by a fast stepping horse. The activity and speed of a Cleveland and his ample power and weight to draw the heaviest loads on rubber-tired vehicles give him great usefulness on a modern farm.

Depreciation on tractors is one of the heavy items of farm expenditure. For a man who works horses and breeds such foals as he requires for replacement there is no obligation to put down large sums of money for new purchases. Fuels and oils for tractors, to say nothing of repairs, have to be purchased with cash. The principal food of horses is grass, which needs be supplemented in the case of Clevelands in hard work only by homegrown oats, and in the case of animals in light or casual work by hay in winter. If farming conditions become much more stringent, these considerations may carry much weight in the future.

Horse talk. Left to right: the author, Mr. Lane, Kestrel's owner.

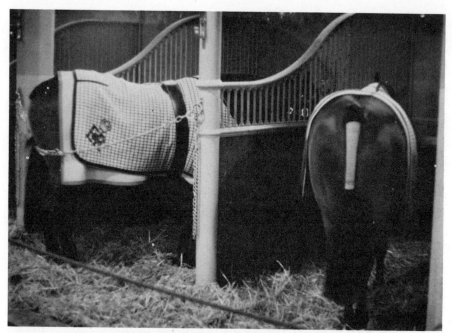

Cleveland Bays in the Royal Mews of Great Britain, London.

The Upgrading of Native Breeds

It has often been said that a Cleveland crossed with a smaller breed will add weight and substance without loss of quality, and crossed with a larger breed will add quality without loss of weight or substance. The truth of this has been recognized all over the world, and is evidenced by the large numbers of Clevelands that have been exported to almost every country for breed improvement.

Hunter Breeding

One of the founders of the Cleveland Bay Horse Society was Mr. Thomas Parrington, father of agricultural shows and hound shows, and one of the leading authorities of his day on agriculture and horse breeding. He swore by Clevelands as the best horse a farmer could use on the land. He was equally emphatic about Cleveland mares being the ideal foundation for producing the best type of bold, weight-carrying hunters, to carry a man 15 to 20 miles to meet hounds, hunt all day, come home with their ears pricked, and do this two or three days a week.

In England it is generally admitted that Cleveland Bay sires produce the very type of mares to mate with premium thoroughbred stallions to produce the best weight-carrying hunters. In this connection the value of a fixed type, as opposed to an unknown quantity, is obvious, especially when the fixed type has the quality of bone and other essential attributes to successful hunter breeding.

But let us not forget that the Cleveland Bay is first of all a coach horse — par excellence. With the current revived interest in driving, the Cleveland Bays are certain to once again return to popularity.

Both coaching and the Cleveland Bays in particular received a tremendous stimulation in interest recently when Prince Philip, Duke of Edinburgh, took his place on the box of a carriage at the Royal Windsor Horse Show. By so doing, he brought to the attention of the entire equestrian world his interest in driving as a sport. As Prince Philip handled the reins over a pair of spanking bay coach horses in competition with some of the best reinsmen in the world his presence lifted driving for pleasure — be it in competition or alone in a shaded lane — high among the various enjoyments of men and horses.*

Even as Prince Philip has long enhanced the game of polo with his skill and enthusiasm, so he seems destined now to bring the driving events before the world's sporting people. The familiar pictures of the British Royal family are as set among wheels and harness as they are in cavalry and parade saddle trappings. Thus the obvious enthusiasm of the Queen and Prince Philip for driving give rise to the belief that the sport will expand at a rapid pace. Also, the fact that, as president of the Federation Equestriene Internationale, he presides over the rules-making body of driving, as well as grand prix, three-day and dressage competitions, further highlights his involvement.

Prince Philip's competitive appearance at the Royal Windsor resulted in mass news media coverage on both sides of the Atlantic with the enthusiastic and affectionate treatment the British Royal family engenders. And almost without exception every news mention of Prince Philip at the Royal Windsor included the fact that he was driving a pair of Cleveland Bays!

*Adapted in part from: J.W. Lane Jr., "Return of the Bays," *The Carriage Journal*, Vol. 10, No. 4, Spring 1973.

3
The Friesian

The Province of Friesland juts north in the Netherlands at about 6° W and 53°N, between the Zuider Zee and the western part of Germany. It seems almost strange that so many wonderful horses come from this general and rather small area. On the German side of this border we have the home of the Oldenburg and the Holstein, while on the Netherlands side, or western side of the border, lies the home of the Groningen, the Gelderland, and the Friesian. The productivity of this horse country does not seem strange, however, when one considers other great horse producing areas lying near 53° North latitude — the northern part of England to the west, and Germany, Poland, and Russia to the east. Add to that the famous Netherlands meadows and rich sandy soil of the Friesland area and you have the basic ingredients to produce good horse flesh and bones.

Of the above mentioned three breeds of horses from the Netherlands I am including here only the Friesian. Not that I am being discriminatory, but I simply cannot include all breeds, as in the manner of an encyclopedia. The Friesian is certainly representative of the type of horse indigenous to this area. That the noble Friesian is exceptional, however, is unquestionable.

The Friesian horse played a dramatic role in a near tragedy which took place some 60 years ago. Just before World War I, this find breed faced extinction. In fact, the number of stallions was reduced to three. A committee was formed, and by careful breeding the Friesian was kept

A pair of Friesian stallions driven to a Friesian Chaise in traditional harness. (Photo by Melissen, Grijpskerk).

A typical Friesian. Note the heavy mane and tail. (Photo by Melissen, Grijpskerk).

Princess Beatrix of the Netherlands being helped into a very ornate vehicle at a Friesian horse show. (Photo by Melissen, Grijpskerk).

The white on the vehicle, on the harness, and even white reins give sharp contrast to the always black Friesian horses. (Photo by Melissen, Grijpskerk).

The Dutch are understandably proud of their Friesian horses. (Photo by Melissen, Grijpskerk).

alive, and today he is just as picturesque and useful as he was in the Middle Ages.*

The Friesian's popularity is based largely on the horse's admirable character. It excels in docility, willingness, and cheerful temperament. These are particularly important characteristics these days when skilled horse handlers are a scarce commodity and many fine horses are subjected to unskilled horsemanship, which might prove risky with horses of less patience and even temperament.

It is said, one never sees a Friesian in poor condition. This may be attributable in some cases more to the Friesian's ability to keep his condition on rations which would starve some breeds, than to the generosity of his keeper. But add a glossy black coat (they are always black, with only a small star permitted) to naturally beautiful conformation and the observer is always in for a thrill.

A finely chiselled head with small ears is carried on a shapely neck with an exceptionally long mane, which has been known to reach the ground. The back is strong, and the ribs deep and well-rounded, though the tail, which carries much hair, is set rather low. This also sometimes reaches the ground. The legs also are heavily covered with hair

*Daphne Machin Goodall, *Horses of the World* (N.Y.C., MacMillan Co., 1965).

A four-in-hand to a Friesian chaise. (Photo by Melissen, Grijpskerk).

Keeping in step for a gala occasion. (Photo by Melissen, Grijpskerk).

sometimes right up to the knee. Neither docking nor trimming of the mane or tail is tolerated in the Friesian horse, and would bar registration in the Friesian Stud Book, which was founded in 1879.*

The Friesian has also been referred to simply as the Dutch. Another name that has been given it is the Harddraver, a title which may be roughly translated as "hard trotter."

Prior to being entered in the Stud Book, the stallions and mares have to comply with high standards of conformation and pedigree. Purity of breed is of major importance. After a special examination they are submitted to a strict veterinary inspection.

During the years of World War II breeding activities greatly increased, since during this time all sorts of activities were put in the way of mechanization. The efficient management of the Stud Books and the excellent breeding material available made it possible to create a large horse population of a quality even better than before.

Because of its impressive color, its tractability, and natural balanced carriage, the Friesian stallion has lately become popular as a circus horse, and it is claimed that the demand is ever increasing.

*Adapted in part from: R.S. Summerhays, *The Observer's Book of Horses and Ponies* (London, Frederick Warne and Co., 1958).

Princess Beatrix of the Netherlands adds the final touch to a glorious day in Friesland. (Photo by Melissen, Grijpskerk).

Princess Beatrix thanks the happy driver for a splendid ride. (Photo by Melissen, Grijpskerk).

Princess Beatrix alights from her totally Friesian drive. (Photo by Melissen, Grijpskerk).

Two Friesians which now make their home in Ohio.

As a nation the Dutch have always been very attracted to the harness horse in the show ring. It is a frequent and popular spectacle to see in the ring Friesian horses drawing Friesian gigs, the occupants perhaps being a gentleman with his lady, both in old Friesian costumes, while to complete the picture the Friesian National Anthem is played.

4

The Hackney

The name of this breed immediately distinguished it. The word "hackney" is very old, extending back over a thousand years; and also its abbreviation "hack," derived from the Latin, have both been used in almost all civilized countries, in some form, to denote both a general purpose horse and the vehicles which he draws.* Crystallizing in modern England, the term was there applied specifically to a type of harness horse midway between the light and heavy sorts. This horse was also much used for riding in early days. It might be described as a heavier strain of the old-time "Norfolk Trotter," because of its origin in the county of Norfolk in England. The two adjoining counties of Norfolk and Suffolk are the most easterly of England and are directly opposite the "Low Countries" (Belgium and Holland) which were the region where the "Great Horse" and other heavy breeds of Europe were evolved in the so-called Dark Ages. In Norfolk, (which is the northern of the two counties), by a refining process, brought about by a crossing-in of thoroughbred blood, the Norfolk Trotter and his derivative, the Hackney, were produced. In Suffolk, on the other hand, was produced the Suffolk Punch, in which the draft type reached extreme development.

The Hackney, as a distinct type, did not emerge until comparatively recent times. Its patriarch (i.e., most important sire in its development

*Adapted in part from: Dinsmore and Hervey: *Our Equine Friends* (Horse and Mule Association of America, 1944).

The Hackney. (Sculpture by Eustis).

Grand Champion Hackney, Marden Midas.

Mr. Chauncey Stillman driving Lawton gig, with Groom Richard Belliveau, at the Royal Winter Fair Horse Show, Toronto. The horse is Brook-Acres Silver Vision.

Mrs. Frank Haydon driving a unicorn (three horses, one in front of two) of hackney horses to a shooting brake, with Grooms Richard Belliveau, and Maurice St. George, at the Royal Winter Fair Horse Show, Toronto. The horses are; Brook-Acres Silver Vision, leader; Marden Ambassador, wheeler; and Hurstwood Vodka, wheeler.

Standard Bred horse drawing a George IV phaeton at Morven Park, Leesburg, Va.

Cross-bred horse drawing a sulky at Morven Park, Leesburg, Va.

A Morgan drawing a sulky at Morven Park, Leesburg, Va.

into a breed) is commonly assigned as being Blaze (foaled 1733), grandson of the Darley Arabian – the same Blaze from whom imported Messenger, the patriarch of the American Standard Bred trotter, was also directly descended. The Hackney became specialized for use in the British hackney-coaches of the 18th century, and, as a type, was later consecrated to the use of the upper classes in their road driving, hitched to vehicles of many kinds. As such they were bred with that object in view calling for an animal of more robust conformation than those used for racing purposes, yet of high finish, symmetry and speed, with especially flashy action at the trot. The size aimed at was medium to small, with roundness of outline and jaunty carriage, in height from something under 15 hands to not more than 15.2, and in weight from 900 to 1,100 pounds. Bay, brown, and chestnut are the preferred colors. Hackneys were, before the advent of the carriage, used under saddle and also were employed for some light agricultural work.

Prior to the coming of the automobile, Hackneys were much in demand and were actively promoted in England, with a stud book of their own and strong publicity. Many choice individuals were imported into America, chiefly for show and "fancy" driving and for breeding

Mrs. Frank Haydon driving a basket phaeton at the Devon Horse Show with Groom, Maurice St. George. The horses are Ardkinglas Marques, and Brook-Acres Silver Vision.

Miss Elizabeth Stillman being driven to the church for her wedding July 2, 1966, in postillion driven George IV Phaeton accompanied by her father, Chauncey Stillman. The lead pair is ridden by Victor Shone, and the wheel pair is ridden by Richard Belliveau. The horses are Stillman hackneys.

Mr. Chauncey Stillman driving Marden Wracksul and Marden Ambassador in a "sailor wagon," attended by Richard Belliveau.

Barouche drawn by a pair, postillion ridden by Richard Belliveau at Stratford, Virginia. The passengers are Mrs. Claude Lancaster, Hon. and Mrs. Reginald Wynn, and the Host is Chauncey Stillman. Mr. Maurice St. George is in the rumble seat. The horses are Impromptu and Wethersfield Lysander.

HRH Prince Philip, Duke of Edinburgh, opening the Royal Winter Fair Horse Show in Toronto, 1966. He is in the same equipage that Elizabeth Stillman rode to her wedding in.

67

Mrs. Frank Haydon driving unicorn hitched to a shooting brake at the Royal Winter Fair Horse Show, Toronto. The horses are; Brook-Acres Silver Vision, leader; Marden Ambassador, wheeler; and Marden Wracksul, wheeler.

Mrs. Frank Haydon driving Marden Wracksul and Brook-Acres Silver Vision hitched in tandem to a Lawten gig at the Royal Winter Fair Horse Show, Toronto.

Miss Sidney Smith driving Marden Ambassador hitched to a viceroy at the Devon Horse Show, near Philadelphia.

purposes. And today the Hackney is the most prominent breed of heavy harness or carriage horses in the world.

One of the earliest Hackneys to be brought to America was a stallion named Pretender, a great grandson of a horse called Old Shales, imported to Virginia in 1801. Later importations followed but the breed was slow to catch on in America, primarily because the conditions of the frontier roads did not permit the Hackney to show his qualities to advantage. Toward the end of the century greater numbers were brought over. They seemed to fit well into the Gay Nineties and the Gas Light Era, when prancing carriage horses became characteristic of the avenues traveled by the wealthy in the eastern cities.

The most common colors found in the Hackney breed are chestnut, bay, and brown, although some roans and blacks are seen. Regular white marks are rather common and are even desired for purposes of accentuating high action. In the show ring, custom decrees that heavy harness horses be docked and have their manes pulled.*

*Adapted in part from: M.E. Ensminger, *Horses and Horsemanship* (Interstate Printers, Danville, Ill., 1951).

Mrs. Frank Haydon driving Ardkinglas Marques and Brook-Acres Silver Vision to a basket phaeton at the Devon Horse Show. Maurice St. George is in the rumble seat.

Mrs. Frank Haydon driving a pair to a "Gooch Wagon" (form of show phaeton) at the Royal Winter Fair Horse Show, Toronto. The horses are Marden Ambassador and Marden Wracksul.

Mr. Chauncey Stillman driving Marden Ambassador and Marden Wracksul to a sailor wagon at Wethersfield with Richard Belliveau in attendance.

In size, the Hackney varies more than any other breed, ranging from 12 to 16 hands. The small Hackney pony, under 14.2 hands in height, and the larger animals are registered in the same stud book. When used in a pair for a lady's phaeton, smaller animals are preferred. Because of the weight of the vehicle, however, a larger animal is necessary when driven singly. As would be expected with the wide range in height, Hackneys vary considerably in weight, from 800 to 1,200 pounds.

Typical Hackneys are relatively short-legged horses, rather robust in conformation; heavy in porportion to their height; smooth and gracefully curved in form, with symmetry and balance; up-headed, clean-cut, alert, and stylish to a high degree. High natural action — which is accentuated by skilled training, bitting and shoeing — is perhaps their most distinguishing feature. The original Hackneys did not have the exaggerated high step — instead they were known for their long, strong stride.

Animals of piebald (black and white) or skewbald (brown and white) color are not eligible for registry.

During the first decade of the 20th century, Alfred G. Vanderbilt, one of the Vanderbilt heirs, regularly made the society pages and sporting publications with his coaching activities. He and his fellow man-about-town, James H. Hyde, set somewhat of a coaching record in 1901 by driving 224 miles from New York to Philadelphia and return in 19 hours and 35 minutes. Although we know Mr. Hyde used his own road coach, specially made for him in Paris, we do not know what kinds of horses were used. There is a good chance they were Hackneys, for Hyde

Centurion by Marden Midas out of Craignorton Lorna Doon, Grand Champion at the Royal Winter Fair Horse Show, Toronto, the past three years.

Mr. Chauncey Stillman driving a small phaeton drawn by the horses, Impromtu and Wethersfield Lysander. His guest is Mrs. Sidney Legendre, and the grooms are Richard Belliveau and Maurice St. George.

Mr. Chauncey Stillman driving the original "Doon" team of bay hackneys imported in 1961 and here hitched to a body brake. On the box seat is stud groom John Goodwin. Riding behind is Miss Mary Theodora Stillman. (Autumn, 1961)

Mr. Chauncey Stillman winning pair class at the Devon Horse Show, June, 1971, with Marden Ambassador and Marden Wraksul.

Marden Wracksul and Marden Ambassador, owned by Mr. Chauncey Stillman and driven here by Mr. Richard Belliveau the manager at Wethersfield Stable, Amenia, N.Y., June, 1969.

Mr. Chauncey Stillman driving a four-in-hand team to a park drag, 1971.

A tandem hitch of Hackneys to a "going to cover" cart. (Sculpture by Eustis).

favored them. In fact, he regularly drove to his office in his hansom, drawn by a tall, black Hackney, which always had violets attached to its bridle to match the dapper master's boutonniere.

It is interesting to note how brief was the career of both these young men. Although Hyde had inherited controlling interest in the Equitable Life Assurance Society upon the death of his father he never seriously assumed the business responsible for his great wealth. For personal reasons Hyde withdrew to France and obscurity in 1905. Vanderbilt, on the other hand, lost his life in the sinking of the Lusitania in 1915. For the duration, however, the exploits of these gentlemen added an exciting flavor to the history of coaching in this country.

5
The Hanoverian

The Hanoverian breed of horse, from the vicinity of the City of Hanover in Germany, is one of the best known breeds in Europe and is well over 200 years old. Referred to as Hanover's Noble Warmblood, the horses of this breed always place in the first positions in the large exposition of the German Agricultural Society.

Purebred Hanoverian families are the basis for the different refinements of the breed. The Hanoverian combines nobility with size and strength as hardly any other horse in the world. To preserve hardiness, expression, and beauty the Hanoverian families are combined frequently with special bloodstreams in cautious proportions. These enter the breed by stallions of the Thoroughbred, Arabian, and East Prussian breeds. The crossing of English Thoroughbreds with the existing German horses of some two hundred years ago started the Hanoverian breed as it is known today.

These old German breeds originated from the German Great Horse of the Middle Ages, which was a descendant of the horses that carried the Franks under Charles Martel, when they met and defeated the Saracens at the Battle of Poitiers in A.D. 732, one of the decisive battles of the world. The descent of these animals may be traced from the Eastern and Southern European breeds of pre-Christian times, mixed with the horses of the Tencteri, a German tribe who settled on the left bank of the Rhine River about A.D. 100. The Tencteri were distinguished from all other German tribes by their love of horses and their well organized cavalry.

Hanoverian mares at the farm of Otto Enders, Grönloh, Germany.

Hanoverian breeding farm of Otto Enders, Grönloh, Germany.

Alwin Schockemöhle on "Freiheer."

A show of Hanoverian mares.

Olympic riders on Hanoverian horses—H.G. Winkler, Alwin Schockemøhle, and Hermann Schridde.

Meadow idyll in the Lüneburg heather.

From the time of the Franks, the German horse developed and became the great war horse of European armoured chivalry. With the advent of gunpowder, however, and the disappearance of armour, the German breeders saw the need to change the type, and there followed the development of the 17th and 18th century light and heavy cavalry horses. These fell into three main groups – Hanoverian, Mecklenburg, and Danish.

It was this old Hanoverian breed which was interbred with English horses, Arabian, and others, and finally disappeared about the middle of the 18th century. This was replaced by the modern Hanoverian, a close and direct descendant of the famous progenitors of the Thoroughbred, the Darley and Godolphin Arabians and the Byerly Turk.

Today's Hanoverian is a handsome animal, heavily built but with plenty of "blood" about it, powerful quarters and shoulders, thick neck, intelligent head, and good clean legs. The lighter type horses are used for riding and the heavy type horses for harness. As to the color, chestnuts predominate but bay, black, and gray are also seen. In height these horses vary from 16 to 17 hands.

Today the Hanoverian represents in number the largest light-horse breed in Europe. There are more than 8,500 registered mares, often going back 12 to 15 generations. Almost all of the mares are in the possession of farmers in the marshes of the Elbe, Weser, and Aller Rivers, the North Sea coast, and the dry Hanoverian uplands.

A trotter (left) next to a galloping horse (right).

Double-driving school.

Six-horse-hitch on a manor coach.

Three year olds taking their tests at Celle.

Freegoing dressage.

There are 160 state stallions of international quality in the state stud at Celle, some 20 miles northeast of Hanover. In the spring the stallions are sent to about 60 service stations for covering the more than 8,500 registered mares.

In Verden, about 45 miles north-northwest of Hanover, and on the same Aller River that flows past Celle, is the large sales and auction center. Here, twice a year, in spring and fall, are held the famous Hanoverian auctions. Although the Hanoverian has retained his re-

Old Roman chariot with four abreast.

markable ability to perform superbly in harness, one may now find in this breed anything from a heavy-weight hunter to an extravagant dressage horse; from first class breeding material to a top show jumper. In the breeding region of Hanover one can find everything in a large assortment. The Hanoverian's capacity is proverbial and it does not have any problems of acclimatization. The part of Hanoverian horses in olympic successes is not only dominating within the German breeds, but the Hanoverian is right in front in the teams for the Prix de Nations as well as the Prix de Dressage with international participation.

Many German breeds are based on Hanoverian blood, and in foreign countries such as Belgium, Czechoslovakia, Denmark, Great Britain, The Netherlands, Canada, Luxembourg, Austria, Sweden, Switzerland, South-West Africa, USSR, USA, and several countries of Latin America, Hanoverians are used for breeding.

Hartwig Steenken and "Simona."

The author admiring a Hanoverian mare at Seabrook Farm, Salem, N.J., December 30, 1974. (Photo by the author's son, Jeffrey S. Jepsen.)

An interesting note concerns the Hanoverian symbol shown at the head of this chapter. This stylized H appears on stables throughout this breed's home country and is always prominently displayed at Hanoverian shows and sales. It is also used as a brand on registered Hanoverians.

Another indication of the esteem with which the German people regard their famous horses from the country south of the Elbe River is the occasional gable-ends seen on barns in and around this region. Being an extension of the end rafters, the distinctive twin horses' heads silhouetted against the sky declare unmistakably this farm is or was the home of Hanoverians.

6
The Morgan

The Morgan has been known as the first family of American horses. The early development of the breed took place in the New England states, thus giving the eastern section of the country primary credit for founding three light-horse breeds, the Morgan, the American Saddle Horse, and the American Standard Bred Trotter.*

The origin of the Morgan breed was a mere happenstance, and not the result of planned effort on the part of breeders to produce a particular breed of horse which would be adapted to local conditions. Whatever may be said of the greatness of Justin Morgan, he was the result of a chance mating — one of nature's secrets for which there is no breeding formula. In fact, it may be said that had a British colonel downed his liquor in his own parlor and had a Springfield, Massachusetts farmer been able to pay his debts, the first family of American horses might never have existed. Legend has it that, one evening during the Revolutionary War, a Colonel Delancey, commander of a Tory mounted regiment, rode up to an inn at King's Bridge. After hitching his famous stallion, True Briton, to the rail, went into the inn for some liquid refreshments, as was his custom. While the Colonel was celebrating with liquor and song, the Yankees stole his horse, later selling the animal to a farmer near Hartford, Connecticut. The whimsical story goes on to say that True Briton later sired the

*Adapted in part from: M.E. Ensminger, *Horses and Horsemanship* (Interstate Printers, 1951).

87

The Brighton Challenge Trophy was won in 1971 and 1972 by Mr. and Mrs. J. Cecil Ferguson's team of Broadwall Morgans. The Fergusons also won the championship driving trophy, and are shown here in the driver's seat. Guests are Mrs. Lois A. Miller and Mr. and Mrs. Davis.

fuzzy-haired colt that was to be christened after his second owner, Justin Morgan. (Morgan first called the horse Figure.)

According to the best authorities, Mr. Morgan, who first lived for many years near Springfield, Massachusetts, moved his family to Randolph, Vermont, in 1788. A few years later, he returned to Springfield to collect a debt. But instead of getting the money, he bartered for a three-year-old gelding and a two-year-old colt of Thoroughbred and Arabian extraction. The stud colt, later named after the new owner, as was often the custom of the day, became the noted horse, Justin Morgan, the progenitor of the first famous breed of horses developed in America.

Justin Morgan was a dark bay with black legs, mane, and tail. His head was shapely; his dark eyes were prominent, lively, and pleasant; his wide-set ears were small, pointed, and erect; his round body was short-backed, close-ribbed, and deep; his relatively thin legs were set wide and straight, and the pastern and shoulders were sloping; his action was straight, bold, and vigorous; and his style was proud,

A team of Morgans owned and driven by Mr. Lawrence A. Appley, President of the American Morgan Horse Association. With him in the carriage is his trainer, Mr. Fred Herrick.

A Morgan drawing a two-wheeled gig at Morven Park, Leesburg, Va.

nervous, and imposing. Justin Morgan was a beautifully symmetrical, stylish, vibrant animal — renouned for looks, manners, and substance. It was claimed of him that he could outrun for short distances any horse against which he was matched. He was a fast trotter, a great horse on parade under saddle, and he could outpull most horses weighing several hundred pounds more.

The horse, Justin Morgan, lived his 32 years (1789-1821) in an era of horses rather than an era of power machinery. The westward expansion had been limited; roads and trails were in the raw, as nature had left them, and were often impassable even with a horse and buggy. Virgin forest had to be cleared, and the tough sod of the prairie had to be broken. These conditions called for an extremely versatile type of horse — one that could pull a good load on the farm, could be driven as a roadster, could be raced under saddle, and could be ridden in a parade. Justin Morgan and his progeny filled this utility in a most remarkable manner. In due time, in 1893 to be exact, many years after the death of the foundation sire and after a decade of exhaustive research, one Colonel Joseph Battell published Volume I of the American Morgan Horse Register. Such was the beginning of preservation of the lineage of the breed, a registry assignment now handled under the same name by the Morgan Horse Club.

The famous National Grand Champion Stallion 1955 National Reserve Champion Harness and Saddle Horse. Owned by Mr. and Mrs. J. Cecil Ferguson, Broadwall Farm, Greene, Rhode Island, Parade was guest artist with the Lippizans (white stallions) on their 1964 tour.

Parade and Broadwall Drum Major, the two Morgan stallions who made the famous tour of the United States and Canada with the white stallions (Lippizans) from Vienna. Water color by Harold G. Bruel.

What could be more stylish?

With shifts in use, it is but natural to find considerable variation in the size of present-day Morgans. Yet throughout the vicissitudes of time, and shifts in emphasis that have occurred during the past 100 years, Morgan horses have continued to an amazing degree to have certain unique characteristics which distinquish them as a breed.

The height of representative animals ranges from 14.2 to 16 hands, with the larger animals now given preference by most horsemen. The average Morgan weighs from 800 to 1,200 pounds. Standard colors are bay, brown, black, and chestnut. White markings are not uncommon.

In conformation the breed has retained most of the characteristics attributed to the foundation sire. With greater emphasis on use under saddle, however, modern Morgans are inclined to be more upstanding, have longer necks, and to possess more slope to their shoulders and pasterns. Regardless of type changes, the breed continues to be noted for stamina, docility, beauty, courage, and longevity. The presence of only five lumbar vertebrae in many Morgans is attributed to the use of Arabian breeding.

Lawrence A. Appley, President, American Morgan Horse Association, Inc., driving Applevale Donalect at Saddleback Farm, Hamilton, New York.

Animals with wall-eye (lack of pigment of the iris), or with natural white markings above the knee or hock except on the face, are disqualified for registry.

In the early formative period of the breed, the Morgan was thought of as a general purpose type of animal — for use in harness racing, as a roadster, on the farm, on the avenue, in the park, on the range, and on the trail. It was estimated in 1870 that 90 percent of the horses used in the cities and countryside for pulling carriages, railway streetcars, and coaches were Morgans. With the development of mechanization, many of these needs disappeared. The more progressive breeders, fully aware of the change in needs, took stock of the breed's inherent possibilities and shifted their efforts in breeding and selection to the production of a superior riding horse. At the present time, therefore, it is not surprising to find that there is considerable variation in emphasis in different sections of the United States. In the West, the Morgan is primarily a stock horse; in the central states, it is still a general purpose breed; whereas in the East the emphasis is upon the Morgan as a saddle horse, particularly for general country use and the recreation purposes over the hundreds of miles of trails.

The comparatively small number of purebred Morgans today is no criterion of the true importance of the breed. Their influence has literally extended to the entire horse population of the continent. Morgan blood was used in laying the foundation for many breeds. The leading Standardbred families of today are a fusion of Hambletonian lines with Morgan. Likewise, the American Saddle Horse is indebted to the Morgan, for Peavine and Chief families both contain Morgan ancestry. Allen, the foundation sire of the Tennessee Walking Horse, was a great grandson of a Morgan, Vermont Black Hawk.

During the period of transition and shift in emphasis from a utility and harness type of horse to use under the saddle, the registration of Morgan horses declined, and the identity of many registered animals was lost. This greatly reduced the number of available breeding animals to use as a base for the rapid expansion of breeding interest that has occurred recently.

In 1907, Colonel Battell — an admirer, breeder, and the founder of the Register of Morgan Horses, presented to the United States Department of Agriculture what became known as the U.S. Morgan Horse Farm, near Middlebury, Vermont. Col. Battell's primary objective in presenting the farm to the Federal Government was that of providing a place upon which the breed could be perpetuated and improved. Though it would appear ironical today, it was also rumored that the old gentleman was disturbed by the high taxes of the period and had decided that the only way to beat the Government was to give

Lawrence A. Appley, President, American Morgan Horse Association, Inc., driving Applevale Donalect at Saddleback Farm, Hamilton, New York.

This tranquil scene shows the mare Bald Mt. Trixiefield with her April foal, Bold Prelude, enjoying the warm summer sunshine. Both are owned by the Richard Schmidt family of Fair Haven, Vermont.

If we could use only one word for this turnout, it would be elegant.

Style comes in pony-size, too.

his holdings to the United States. Regardless of the possible latter objective, it must be agreed that the U.S. Morgan Horse Farm was a powerful influence in perpetuating and improving the Morgan breed. On July 1, 1951, by authorization of the U.S. Congress, the U.S. Morgan Horse Farm was transferred without cost to the Vermont Agriculture College.

A Morgan drawing a sulky past the Mansion at Morven Park, Leesburg.

Beauty in motion. Pair of Oldenburgs driven by Mr. Tom Ryder to a Beaufort phaeton at Seabrook Farm, Salem, N.J., December 1974. Author is on the driver's side seat behind the driver. Other members of his family occupy the six-passenger vehicle. (Photo by Jeffrey S. Jepsen)

A nicely matched pair drawing a trap. (Photo by Stanley M. Jepsen)

Beautiful countryside and a most pleasant way to see it. Tom Ryder driving and the author beside him at Seabrook Farm, N.J. (Photo by Jeffrey S. Jepsen)

7

The Oldenburg

The Oldenburg is a German horse somewhat heavier than the Cleveland Bay, and was not available outside Germany until 1968, when a team of greys was purchased for the Queen of England. This is one of the breeds that was strengthened by the Cleveland Bays. Both the Oldenburgs and the Hanoverians were carefully built up in numbers after World War II, when they were badly needed for work on the land. They are now being crossed with Arab and Thoroughbred stallions to produce good quality riding horses.

The Oldenburg was the original breed that brought the German coach horse into prominence. It was developed in the Duchy of Oldenburg on the left bank of the Lower Weser River, west of Bremen, in the district known as the Oldenburg Weser Marsh.*

The breeding district is composed of about two-thirds marsh and one-third moor and "Geest," a somewhat higher lying land the soil of which is chiefly a diluvial deposit and not so fertile as that of the marshes. All these soils combine to make horse breeding profitable in the region as they provide the necessary pasturage to ensure the quick development of the young animals.

This tract of country is very fertile and has been gradually reclaimed from the sea after centuries of labor. High dikes protect the marsh to

*Adapted in part from: *J. Schüssler, *The Oldenburg Horse* (Germany, The . Oldenburg Horse Breeders Society, 1914).

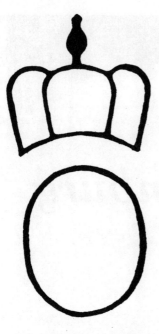

Oldenburg Premium Brand.

Oldenburg Stud-Book Brand.

Author's wife Ruth, and daughter Jenny on right, petting pair of grey Oldenburgs at Seabrook Farm, Salem, N.J. (Photo by Jeffrey S. Jepsen)

Mrs. Tom Ryder harnessing a grey Oldenburg gelding at Seabrook Farm, Salem, N.J. (Photo by Jeffrey S. Jepsen)

the north and east from the inroads of the sea, which every now and then makes renewed efforts to gain back the land which has been rescued from it.

The inland side of the marsh is nearly always bounded by fen which has been cultivated for ages. It is almost equal to the marsh in fertility and is used for the same purposes, namely, as pasture and meadow. In places, the marsh bounds the more hilly "Geest," and here there are beautiful woods, good pastures, and fertile meadows.

A network of canals and smaller ditches is interwoven over the whole drainable extent of the country. In the Weser and the moor marshes these ditches contain fresh water, so that nearly everywhere the stock is able to drink from them.

The climate, because of the proximity of the sea, is a damp one but is not subject to sharp changes in temperature. It is therefore well suited for stock raising. In spring and fall there are often fogs, a heavily clouded sky, and biting winds. On the other hand it is not too warm in summer, and severe cold occurs, but seldom in winter and then for only a short period. One can nearly always figure on an average pasturing season of about seven months, from May to November. This then is the home of the horse which bears the name of his homeland — Oldenburg.

The Oldenburg is a strong, heavy carriage horse. It has a muscular and symmetrical body with good neck, is placed on strong, sinewy legs

Author leading out an eight year old Oldenburg gelding imported from Germany by John Seabrook of Salem, N.J. (Photo by Jeffrey S. Jepsen)

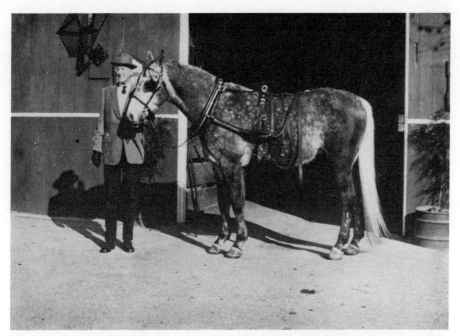

Author and harnessed Oldenburg named Majesty at Seabrook Farm, Salem, N.J. (Photo by Jeffrey S. Jepsen).

Tom Ryder and his wife Joyce hitching up team of Oldenburgs—Majesty (foreground) and Milord (background) to a Beaufort phaeton. Vehicle was designed for a shooting phaeton and used to take Hunters to the cover. (Photo by Jeffrey S. Jepsen)

Oldenburgs from the box seat—Majesty (left) and Milord (right). (Photo by Jeffrey S. Jepsen)

with plenty of bone, and has a high energetic action. The color is brown, dark brown, or black, nearly always a whole color with very few markings. There are also chestnuts and greys, but these are scarce.

The Oldenburg has a robust constitution. He has to thank his upbringing for his hardy character, as he was raised in the open from earliest spring till late in the fall and has to stand the various climatic changes that occur in the vicinity of the North Sea. He has one particular advantage over all other breeds, in that he matures earlier than they do. Mature horses weigh from 1,200 to 1,400 pounds, and average 16 hands in height.

The Oldenburg coach horse resulted from a cross of purebred and half-bred stallions of the "Karossier" or "State Coach Horse" class, with typical Oldenburg mares. It is seldom that an ideal has been so well thought out and carried with such zeal to perfection, as has been the case with the breeding of the Oldenburg horse, hence the uniform type that exists.

The best of these horses have for their origin the famous "Stäveschen Stallion" which was foaled in England in 1806. One must keep in mind, however, that this horse had a splendid foundation for the furtherance of the breed in the mares then existing and also that the State Selecting Commission of those days was very strict in their choice of the animals that were to be used for stud purposes. We have no way of knowing to what blood the mares at that time owed their origin, as nearly all the pedigrees and descriptions of the mares were destroyed by a fire that took place in the Castle of Varel in 1757 where the stud documents were kept. The horses of those days were of the heavy coach horse type, for the Oldenburg historian, von Halem, writing of the times of Count Anton Günther of Oldenburg (1603-1667) says: "The Oldenburg horses were prized by princes and potentates for their size, beauty, and strength."

The "Stäveschen Stallion" was in all probability a half-bred and was bought at Brunswick in 1820 upon the approval of the Selecting Committee. The horse was almost 17 hands high, chestnut brown with a star, "the build, shape, bone, and muscle of the stallion were found to be of exceptionally fine proportions." He was used for only three years in the breeding district, but in that time sired "Neptun," foaled in 1821, and "Thorador," foaled in 1823, and it was these two stallions that became the sires of the most noted progeny.

From the excellent records available from that time to the present, (plus well-substantiated previous history), it is evident that the Oldenburg had its origin in an old race of horses peculiar to the country, which from time to time has been improved by the use of English Thoroughbreds and well-born half-breds. The Oldenburg

Author and family being driven around Seabrook Farm by Tom Ryder. Ruth Jepsen is in the middle seat and the Jepsen's two daughters are in the back seat, facing back, while Jeffrey is taking the picture.

breeders though have never committed the mistake, (as has sometimes happened in other breeds), of allowing their animals to become too "fine" and notwithstanding the judicious use of "Blood." It can still be said that the old "Marsh Horse" has kept its place and has been of the greatest possible use in establishing the present breed.

There is no doubt that the old Marsh Horse has been instrumental in preserving the strong legs, the sinewy muscles, the deep build, the hardy constitution, the even temperament, and the early maturity of the race. It is to these excellent qualities that the Oldenburg owes its popularity and has established an ever increasing demand.

Other "warm" blooded breeds (in Germany particularly, the distinction between "warm" and "cold" blooded is made, the former being used for fast work, and the latter being draft horses) have been gradually getting too fine and to a great extent, nervy. The Oldenburg, on the contrary, has kept his weight and is now acknowledged to be the heaviest "warm" blooded breed in the world.

In no other breeding district, England scarcely excepted, have the breeders held so fast to the type of strong, muscular breeding animals of both sexes to produce a weighty coach or carriage horse, as they have done in Oldenburg. It is owing to this principle that the Oldenburg, in spite of a little inbreeding to consolidate the race, has

Turning into the home gate. (Photo by Jeffrey S. Jepsen)

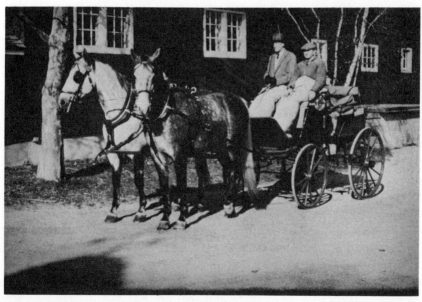

The author, at the reins of team in previous pictures, with Tom Ryder also on the box seat. Mr. Ryder is the author of the driving manual On the Box Seat, *and is one of the world's leading authorities on formal driving. (Photo by Jeffrey S. Jepsen)*

been able to preserve his excellent characteristics.

The Oldenburg has been bred almost entirely by small farmers since time immemorial. They usually have only two brood mares as the farms are not of sufficient size to allow more being kept. The stallions also are in private ownership, as there are no State or other Stud farms in Oldenburg. The mares are sent to the horse farm between March and the end of June.

On an average the stallion covers from 120 to 130 mares. The best stallions are, of course, very much in demand. Notwithstanding the heavy work required of them, they are good producers, some 75% of the mares remaining in foal. When the season is over, the stallions are sent to grass and remain there till the end of September or beginning of October if the weather is suitable. The brood mares, even when at work on the farm, are kept at pasture; if the work is heavy they are fed some corn in addition. Foals stay at grass all summer until late autumn. The young horses are put to light work when they are two years old. They are very tractable and let themselves be easily handled. If one takes ordinary precautions at first, they cannot be said to have any vice. When three years old they are put to all kinds of work and are then also used for breeding purposes.

Owing to the condition of the soil and weather during the winter, the horses come in for a good deal of rest. It is not infrequent that horses that have been constantly at work are then kept entirely in the stable. But this does not have a derogatory effect on their health, as would certainly be the case with an ordinary coach horse. The young animals are mostly kept in box stalls during the winter. In districts where straw is not easily obtainable, moss litter (also called peat-litter) is used and provides a splendid substitute. This is either bought direct from the factory in bales, or where the farmers have peat bogs of their own it is hauled from there. The litter is either torn apart by machinery or is trodden to pieces by the horses themselves.

The Oldenburg horse is a good doer and is nearly always an excellent though rather small feeder. The winter rations are comprised chiefly of hay and oats. The older horses get, on a average, about seven pounds of oats and as much hay a day, and sometimes a little straw. The younger horses get nine to eleven pounds of oats, plenty of hay, and a few mangels, the latter especially for the first few weeks after they have been brought in from grass.

The brood mares, particularly at the latter part of their time, are exercised freely or put to light work. When near foaling they are watched day and night. Some days after the birth of the foal, if the weather is favorable, both mare and foal are put out to grass. At first they are stabled at night, but as soon as the foal is strong enough they are turned out for good.

A four-in-hand of Oldenburgs owned by Her Majesty the Queen of England.

Foals that have been sold are usually weaned at four months, the others remaining with the dam 5 to 7 months. They are then separated from her and the mare returns to her work on the farm.

The chief horse-fairs in the districts are held at Jever, Oldenburg, Ovelgönne, and Varel. Older horses are to be had at all these, whereas the principal fair for yearling colts is the so-called Medardus Market held at Oldenburg at the beginning of June each year. For the 18-months-old fillies and foals of the year the autumn fairs held at Oldenburg, Ovelgönne, and Varel are considered the best. Particular attention, however, is drawn to the fact that at these latter markets most of the horses are already in the possession of horse dealers who have bought the animals and taken them off the hands of the breeders a few days before the fair at places appointed for that purpose. These so-called "early markets" are gaining in importance from year to year. It cannot, therefore, be too strongly impressed on intending purchasers that they should visit these "early markets" so as to see the best that is to be had.

Another good opportunity for buying two-year-olds and younger animals is at the local shows, usually held at the end of summer. The largest and best of these are the ones at Stollhamm, Ovelgönne, Berne, Oldenburg, and Jever.

Each year, at the end of January or beginning of February, the State Selecting Committee has the stallions brought to Oldenburg for selection. In the course of time this has become a recognized opportunity for the sale of the same. On an average about 300 stallions are brought together, amongst which are usually some 250 three-year-olds which, as yet, have not been selected. Buyers for foreign Studs often purchase their rising three-year-olds in early summer or a little later in the year. The first reason being that there are more animals to choose from at that time, and secondly, the horses have more time to get accustomed to their new surroundings before being used for breeding purposes the next spring. This also applies to the American importers, especially as they can make their purchases in France and Belgium about the same time.

If foreign buyers wish to see and buy large numbers of horses without going to the Shows or Horse Fairs for that purpose, the Council of the Stud Book is usually prepared to make arrangements with the breeders to bring their animals to a place where they can be conveniently seen and compared, and to issue private catalogues to make the selection of unrelated horses easier.

Wherever the Oldenburg horse has been exhibited he has always met with astonishing success. It is not only that individual horses have gained honors, but that the collection, as a whole, has been of such

The Queen of England's Oldenburgs in cross country competition.

108

Four of the Queen of England's Oldenburgs. Horses of the lead team clearly show they are related to Mr. John Seabrooks' dapple greys shown elsewhere in the book.

quality as to command attention and surprise.

It seems appropriate to close this chapter with one anecdote to illustrate the esteem with which Oldenburg horses have been held since the earliest times.

In the 17th century, conspicuous colors, beautiful manes and tails were highly prized in horses. Amongst the Oldenburgs, beside browns and blacks with black manes and tails, bright chestnuts with white manes and tails, dappled and pearl colored horses were prevalent.

The favorite charger of the above mentioned Count Anton Günther of Oldenburg, the grey stallion "Kranich," was far-famed. He had a wonderful mane and tail. The mane was 12 feet 10 inches in length and is still shown in Oldenburg. The tail was 16 feet 9 inches long, and is in Copenhagen, Denmark.

8

The Royal Mews of Great Britain

As early as the time of Richard II (1377-1399) there were King's Mews. The word "mews," however, had a different meaning in those days. It derives from the old French word "mue" (from the Latin "mutare"—to change) meaning a changing especially of the coat or skin. A "mews" in the Middle Ages was a place where the King's falcons were kept during their "mewing" or change of plumage.

For centuries the "King's Mews" in London were near Charing Cross on the north side of what is now Trafalgar Square, and until the reign of Henry VIII they were used exclusively for keeping falcons. In 1537 the royal stables which were then in Lomesbury (now called Bloomsbury) were destroyed by fire and Henry had the falcons removed from the mews at Charing Cross and his stud horses were established there.

The Royal Mews were rebuilt in the reigns of Edward VI and Mary I, but by 1732 the buildings were in such a state of disrepair that George II had them pulled down and new stables designed by William Kent the architect were built.

Before passing to the present Royal Mews at Buckingham Palace it is interesting to note that in 1785 strict rules for the gate porter were in force and orders of a very similar nature still apply today. To quote: they were "to suffer no loose, idle, or suspicious persons, or women of the town to lurk or harbour near the Mews, and to shut the gate at ten at night."

Gateway to the Royal Mews as it looks today. (Photo by Jeffrey S. Jepsen)

In 1762 George III bought Buckingham House (later Buckingham Palace) from the Duke of Buckingham, and henceforth the stables were used in addition to those at Charing Cross. The present Riding School, or Riding House, was built under the direction of John Nash in 1764. In 1824, four years after George IV came to the throne, Nash was commissioned to re-design the stables and coach houses, and they became the Royal Mews in 1825—the date shown on the weathervane above the handsome porch.

The Mews consists of a quadrangle entered from Buckingham Palace Road by a Doric archway surmounted by a clock tower. The east side is still occupied by state coaches; and the west and north quarters contain some of the finest stables in existence. They are unaltered except that some stalls have been converted into loose boxes. Behind the quadrangle are more coach houses in which are kept the state and private motor cars. Above these buildings are modernized flats where the married coachmen, grooms, and chauffeurs live.

The Carriage Horses

From the numerous records about horses in the royal archives it would appear that chestnut horses have never been used as harness horses in the Royal Mews. Dun, cream, black, bay, and grey horses have been used roughly in that order since the reign of George II.

The Gold State Coach, built in 1762. (Photo by Jeffrey S. Jepsen)

George I started importing horses from Hanover, Germany, and subsequently large numbers of Hanoverian horses were purchased continuously until well into the present century. Horses have also been brought from France, Spain, Morocco, and Holland.

For many years the most famous royal horses were the Creams, which were introduced into England in 1714 upon the accession of George I. They were then used by the heads of the states of Hanover, Schaumberg-Lippe, and Gotha where the only studs were located. Creams, which were used by the sovereign on occasions of the highest state, were bred at Hampton Court until 1920 when, because of inbreeding and the impossibility of obtaining replacements, their use had to be discontinued.

Blacks were used on important official occasions until the mid-1920s. They were stallions also of Hanoverian origin. They took the place of the Creams for two years and then they were displaced by the Bays.

The Bays, still in use today, are predominantly Cleveland Bays, supplemented by a number of Dutch and Irish horses, and some Oldenburg horses from Germany.

Lastly, and today the most famous are the Windsor Greys. They draw The Queen's carriages, and were used for the coronations of King George VI and Her Majesty. They are not a special breed but from Victorian times and earlier grey horses were always kept at Windsor, and it was not until after the reign of King George V that they were moved to London. In the early days these horses were quite small, almost ponies, and were used mainly for drawing the private driving carriages at Windsor, and thus acquired their title "Windsor Greys."

In addition to harness horses there have always been riding horses in the Royal Stables, although today these are not kept in London. At Windsor Castle there are horses of many types and origins including Arab, Pakistan, Portuguese, and Russian hacks, as well as a number of Argentine polo ponies. These are regularly used by the members of the Royal Family

The Gold State Coach

An entry in the journal kept by the Clerk of the Stables still in the Royal Mews records that at the beginning of the reign of George III a "very superb" State Coach was ordered to be built. Several designs were produced and those selected were put together by Mr. (later Sir William) Chambers, Surveyor of His Majesty's Board of Works.

On November 24, 1762, the journal says that about 5 A.M. that day the new State Coach was brought to the Mews. At 8 A.M. eight cream

Some of the famous Windsor Greys inside The Royal Mews. (Photo by Jeffrey S. Jepsen)

horses were attached to it to try it around the Mews and it was found satisfactory. On the following day the king went to the House of Peers in the new State Coach to open the session of Parliament, and the crowd which turned out to see it was exceedingly great "yet no accident happened but one of the Door Glasses and the handle of the Door being broken!" Later it was recorded that "the new State Coach was the most superb and expensive of any ever built in this Kingdom."

The framework of the body consists of eight palm trees which, branching at their tops, support the roof. The four corner trees, each rising from a Lion's head, are loaded with trophies symbolizing the victories of Great Britain in the Seven Years War that had ended just before the coach was completed.

The body is slung by braces covered in morocco leather and ornamented with gilt buckles held by four tritons. The two front figures draw the coach—cables attached to cranes are stretched over their shoulders—and they proclaim the approach of the Monarch of the Ocean through conches used as horns. The rear figures carry the Imperial fasces topped with tridents.

On the center of the roof stand three cherubs representing the genii of England, Scotland, and Ireland. These support the Royal Crown, and hold in their hands the Scepter, the Sword of State, and the Ensign of Knighthood respectively. Their bodies are draped with festoons of laurel which fall to the four corners of the roof Among the many minor features are the driver's footboard in the shape of a large scallop shell ornamented with bunches of reeds; the pole, representing a bundle of lances; the splinter bar composed of a rich moulding issuing from beneath a large voluted shell with each end terminating in a dolphin's head; and the wheels imitated from those of an ancient triumphal car.

The coach is gilded all over. It is 24 feet long, 8 feet 3 inches wide, and 12 feet high; the pole is 12 feet 4 inches long, and the total weight is four tons. The harness, originally made by Ringstead, is of rich red morocco leather.

The State Coach is adorned on the sides, front, and back with panels painted by Giovanni Battista Cipriani, a Florentine historical painter and engraver who came to London in 1755.

The coach has been used for every coronation since that of George IV and until recent years was generally used when the sovereign went in person to open the new session of Parliament. Queen Victoria, however, opened Parliament only seven times after the Prince Consort's death in 1861, and she did not use the State Coach. Since the Second World War it has been used only for the coronation of The Queen in 1953. It has been overhauled a number of times.

The State Coach takes eight horses to pull it and until the First World War they were always cream Hanoverian stallions, but in 1921 and 1922 black horses were substituted. From 1923 bay horses were regularly used until the coronation of King George VI. Since then grey horses have pulled the coach.

Some of the Royal carriage harness. (Photo by Jeffrey S. Jepsen)

It was originally driven from the box, the first six horses being driven by a coachman and the leading pair being postillion ridden; that is each of the two lead horses carried a rider. King Edward VII had the hammer cloth and box removed as he thought they prevented people from seeing Queen Alexandra and himself, so now it is drawn by eight postillion horses. The State Coach can only proceed at the walk whereas all other coaches in the Royal Mews can be used at the trot.

The Master of the Horse

The office of Master of the Horse in the Royal Household is one of high honor and great antiquity. It ranks next to those of Lord Steward and Lord Chamberlain.

There are numerous references in early history to the office. Tacitus, the Roman historian, refers to the horse "thegn" or "staller" of the Teutonic chiefs as "Comes Stabuli"; the Imperial master of the horse at the time of the Byzantine empire was also known as the "Comes Stabuli." In England, after the Norman conquest, the royal horses were in charge of the "Custodes Equorum Regis" (keepers of the king's horses). In those days the horses were kept as much for war as for the king's personal use. They were distributed among his manors which included Windsor, Guildford, Odiham, Woodstock, and Waltham, but

Detail of Royal carriage harness. (Photo by Jeffrey S. Jepsen)

116

after the Battle of Poitiers in 1356, the war establishment was reduced and many studs were closed and the horses sold. William of Wykeham, as Edward III's "Surveyor of the King's Work in Windsor Castle," received the proceeds and it is reasonable to surmise that the sale of royal horses contributed to the building of the castle.

In 1391, in the reign of Richard II, John Russell was appointed the first "Magister Equitii" (Master of the Horse), and from that time a record exists of every appointment to the office.

The office of Master of the Horse is one whose holder changed with the Government, as is evidenced by the Duke of Dorset's resignation in 1755 because he did not want to embarrass Canning's administration ". . . were I to obtain a place, which on constitutional as well as on other grounds ought to be filled by one fully prepared to support it." In recent times though this practice has ceased, although in the House of Lords the Master of the Horse never sits on the Opposition benches.

In a journal started on November 18, 1760, it is recorded that "No regular office for the Clerk of the Stables being kept in the late reign (George II) it was with great difficulty that any books or papers to give proper light into the business of this department could be procured from the person who did the business in the late reign. Much time was therefore spent in searching for precedents and rules for conducting the affairs of the Master of the Horse, to prevent which in future an office was established in the Mews in which the business of the stables was to be transacted."

A completely new establishment was drawn up in 1783 for the royal stables and for His Majesty's Buckhounds, which were also the responsibility of the Master of the Horse. In 1854 John Richard Groves the late major of the Essex Rifles, was appointed the first Crown Equerry, Secretary to the Master of the Horse, and Superintendent of the Royal Mews. This latter appointment became a separate one in 1859. Subsequently the department of the Master of the Horse was renamed the Royal Mews Department. This was necessary because the Master of the Horse ceased to have executive command over the Royal Mews, but he retained his position as the third great officer of the court and as senior personal attendant to the sovereign on all state occasions when horses were used.

The present Master of the Horse, the tenth Duke of Beaufort, was appointed in 1936 and has held office longer than any of his predecessors. He has served four sovereigns and has brought the utmost distinction to his office since he is widely recognized as one of the greatest judges of a horse. Although Her Majesty's Buckhounds no longer exist it is interesting to note that the last person to hunt foxhounds in Windsor Great Park was the Master of the Horse at the beginning of World War II when he was serving at Windsor with the Royal Horse Guards (The Blues).

The introduction of the motor car brought additional responsibilities to the Royal Mews Department for it is concerned with all matters of travel by road. The Crown Equerry is responsible for the motor cars as well as the horses except those in the thoroughbred studs and racing stables, and so the royal cars are accommodated in the Royal Mews.

Liveries and Harness

There are different liveries for State, Semi-State, and everyday occasions. In State Livery a coachman wears a magnificent and very heavy scarlet and gold frock coat, with scarlet plush knee breeches, pink silk stockings, gold buckled shoes, and a wig and tricorne hat decorated with ostrich feathers. His Semi-State Livery is a scarlet frock coat with blue plush knee breeches, white stockings, and a gold-laced top hat. Everyday livery is similar except that buckskin breeches and top boots or a black frock coat are worn.

Postillions also wear a scarlet and gold jacket, wig, and cap for state occasions. For the Ascot processions a scarlet, purple, and gold jacket like the Queen's racing colors is worn. Their Semi-State livery consists of a dark blue jacket with gilt buttons and gold-laced top hat. Everyday

The Royal Mews from Buckingham Palace Road. (Photo by Jeffrey S. Jepsen)

dress is a black jacket and top hat. Postillions always wear buckskin breeches and top boots.

Scarlet cloaks and mackintoshes, and drab boxcloth coats are worn during cold and wet weather.

The collection of harness in the Royal Mews is probably the finest in existence. It includes many sets of superb and historic State Harness and in addition there is Barouche, Clarence, and Brougham Harness. There is also the Postillion Harness known as the Ascot Harness. This bears the Windsor ornamentation, as once differing sets of harness were used for the country and for London, but these have now been merged.

The State Harness consists of eight different sets, each one identified by a name. No. 1 State Harness is used only with the State Coach; No. 2 is the Black Horse State Harness; No. 3 The Queen's (because it is generally used with the Queen's State carriage), and so on. All is very richly decorated with many brass ornaments, except for No. 1, on which all the ornaments are gilt.

Since the State Coach was built in 1762, several sets of harness have been made for it. The first set seems to have been used in November 1774, for the Opening of Parliament. Another set was used for the first time in January 1792. Part of this is still in the Royal Mews.

The eight sets of red morocco State Harness in use today were made in 1834, but they were not used until 1840 when Queen Victoria dined with the Lord Mayor of London soon after her marriage. Each set weighs about 110 pounds and is very richly ornamented with gilt ormolu.

9

The Golden Coach
of the Netherlands

'She comes . . . .
'Drawn with a team of little atomies
'Athwart men's noses as they lie asleep;
'Her waggon-spokes made of long spinner's legs;
'The cover, of the wings of grasshoppers;
'Her traces, of the smallest spider's web;
'Her collars, of the moonshine's wat'ry beams;
"Her whip, of cricket's bone, the lash, of film.'

Such is Shakespeare's description of the ride of Queen Mab, the Queen of the Fairies. Her coach, product of the vivid imagination of one of the world's greatest poets, belongs to the realm of dreams and fantasy. A fairy-tale coach.

But there is another coach that might equally have come straight out of a fairy-tale, a coach of pure gold—the State coach presented by the city of Amsterdam to Queen Wilhelmina on September 7, 1898, as a mark of homage upon her inauguration as Queen of the Netherlands.

This fairy-tale had become a reality through the initiative of the "Friends of the House of Orange," a small group of people in a modest district of Amsterdam. The beginning was through the enthusiasm with which their plan was embraced by the entire population of the city.

The Golden Coach with its eight horse hitch.

The plan then had to be executed. This again was made possible through the generosity of the people of Amsterdam and through the united efforts of the people of the Netherlands, in their resolve to afford the young Queen a worthy token of their loyalty on the occasion of the solemn ceremony that was to reaffirm the ties between the House of Orange and its subjects. It was achieved through the painstaking efforts of smiths and wood-carvers, through the patient needlework of girls in orphanages and elderly ladies in sewing circles, through the consummate skill of painters, glass-blowers and tanners, of gilders and weavers, and craftsmen in ivory and bronze.

Lavish use of materials from both the Motherland and the Overseas Territories was used; flax from Zeeland and leather from Brabant; teak from Java; ivory from Sumatra; gold and silver from far-flung mines. Dutch art, Dutch industry, and Dutch labour all combined to make the fairy-tale come true.

There it stands then, the GOLDEN COACH, drawn by eight horses. On the box, upholstered in royal red edged with gold braid, sits the coachman; on the rear platform stand two grooms in livery. 'The wheels are suns,' writes Anne Mulder in her "History of the House of Orange," 'the spokes golden rays, the rims silver circles adorned with the signs of the Zodiac.' It sounds like a fairy-tale, but it is real.

How did Amsterdam hit on the idea of a ceremonial coach? That is easy to explain. The year is 1898, the motor-car is still a rarity, and the State coach is the traditional royal conveyance. The Queen of England's glass coach was famous, as were the coaches (decorated by celebrated

121

The Queen and Queen Mother alight from the Golden Coach.

painters) of Pope Paul V and Catherine II of Russia. The Czars possessed coaches whose interiors were encrusted with diamonds and other precious stones. For the coronation of Charles X of France a coach had been built at fabulous expense and weighing nearly seven tons. The coach the French Government placed at the disposal of the Emperor of All Russia during his visit to Paris in 1897 was so magnificent that it was never used again but preserved in a museum.

Building such coaches obviously demanded a high degree of craftsmanship, and Amsterdam had long been renowned as a coach-building center. The famous State coaches, which the Dutch Government placed at the disposal of Ambassadors were accredited to the Court of Orange-Nassau, and also the splendid carriages of the City Fathers built in Amsterdam. Foreign kings and princes also commissioned the master-craftsmen of Amsterdam to build their coaches. From Amsterdam came coaches for the Great Elector of Brandenburg and the magnificent Dutch coach ordered by Queen Elizabeth of England.

It is not surprising then, that the city decided to give Queen Wilhelmina a State coach. Nor is it surprising that the city had to mobilize its most skilled craftsmen for the purpose, for this was no ordinary task. The design of the vehicle involved great problems, which the builders, the firm of Spijker, had to solve. The coach had to be so constructed as to afford the queen a clear view of her people and the people a clear view of their queen. The roof had to be high enough to enable the queen to stand up in the coach, yet low enough to enable the coach to pass under medieval arches and the like. Allowance also had to be made for the coach to travel at walking-pace on ceremonial occasions and for the constant reining of the horses. We moderns tend to forget that riding in coaches of this kind, suspended as they were by straps from a double set of springs, was like travelling by ship in a heavy swell. A way had to be found to prevent the royal occupants from becoming seasick! Another difficulty was that the long shaft connecting the front and rear axles under the center of the vehicle made it virtually impossible for the coach to negotiate sharp corners, so it could be driven on straight, wide roads only. That would never have satisfied the people of Amsterdam. As the presentation committee put it: "We want to see our queen riding in our coach through the streets of our city." A solution to the problem had to be sought. The one eventually adopted was an ingenious system incorporating two longitudinal members running along either side of the carriage instead of a single central shaft underneath it. This system not only achieved the desired result but offered two further advantages in that it improved the appearance of the coach and provided a more rigid support for the folding steps; they could now be fixed to one of the side members instead of to the running-boards as they usually were. Anyone who has stepped into a horse-drawn carriage knows that as soon as any weight is put on the steps the whole body will tilt. With a vehicle the size of the Golden Coach the effect would have been magnified several times if the steps had been fixed in the conventional way.

There were a host of other problems, too. Indeed, there is no telling how many blue-prints had to be rejected before the designers were finally able to lean back with a sigh of relief and say that the plans were ready.

Then came the decoration of the coach, which was a problem in itself. The painting was entrusted to Professor N. v.d. Waay of the State Academy of Art, and the groups of figures were designed by Van den Bossche and Crevels. Agreement was reached after lengthy conferences and discussions, after much designing and re-designing. For the coach was meant to represent and illustrate so much. In order to symbolize and express in allegorical form all the blessings and good wishes the Dutch people wanted to shower upon their queen, all the ancient emblems and legendary figures, (to say nothing of practically every representative of the plant and animal kingdoms), had to be pressed into service. Yet they all had to be combined to form a harmonious whole. The coach, in the Dutch Rennaissance style—the style of the most glorious period in Holland's history—had to be a work of art, pleasing to the eye and not overadorned, each part harmonizing with the rest yet conveying its individual message in its own tongue. This we find in the suns painted on the wheelhubs, symbols of a glittering yet benevolent monarchy. The spokes represented the sun's rays shining out in all directions and ending in the firmament with the signs of the zodiac, portrayed on the wheel-rims. We see it on the hinges and door handles, which have dog and owl emblems as symbols of Loyalty and Vigilance. We see the art work in the gay little figures of children who seem almost to be flying ahead of the coach, and in the grim, watchful lions which form a chain of protection at the back of the coach. We see it too in the water-lilies, symbols of Prudence, painted on the steps, and in the birds, symbols of Swiftness, which support the coachman's box.

The decoration on each of the four panels of the coach represented something different. The front panel symbolizes the future. What hopes did the future hold out in 1898? The panel is also very instructive. On the right is a painting representing "Education for the People." On the left "Justice, protecting the needy," showing an injured laborer, an old

The Glass Coach. This 148 year old coach, built in Brussels in 1826, was long used on State occasions in which since 1901, the Golden Coach has been used. The undercarriage is white and gilt, the body dark blue with gilt edges. The side, front, and rear panels are emblazoned with the Royal Coat of Arms. Around the top of the body of the coach is a border painted in various colors and protected by glass—hence the name The Glass Coach. The interior of the coach is upholstered in red velvet and white satin. The State Coat of Arms is embroidered into the center of the roof lining. On the roof, resting on a red velvet cushion, glitters a gilt crown, guarded by four brass lions—one on each corner. The last time The Glass Coach was used was at the marriage of HRH Princess Juliana and HRH the Prince of the Netherlands. On that occasion it was occupied by HM Queen Wilhelmina and HSH Princess Armgard, the Prince's mother.

124

blind man, a widow and orphan children. The hope of social reform springs to mind, old-age pensions, health and safety laws, insurance payments for widows and orphans. Below these pictures is a bas-relief representing "The Benefit of Life Insurance." The right side of the coach depicts a "Tribute from the Netherlands" and the left "Tribute from the Colonies." In the Tribute from the Netherlands we see a central figure, the personification of the Netherlands and the House of Orange. The figure is flanked on one side by Peace, Education, Commerce, Industry, and Agriculture and on the other side by Music, Poetry, Science, Art, and Justice, and guided by Wisdom and supported by Military Power, Discipline, and Order. The Tribute of the Colonies is expressed by the Maid of the Netherlands, flanked on both sides by the sons and daughters of the realm overseas offering gifts. The background on the right is a distant view of the East Indies, and that on the left the West Indies.

The back of the coach is intended to portray "History." It shows a view of Amsterdam in the background, with the Palace on the Dam and the New Church, and in the distance shipping on the River Y and the Amstel. In the foreground the Muse of History immortalizes in the Book of Time the homage of the people to Queen Wilhelmina at the time of her inauguration.

A group of allegorical figures representing the four activities on which the prosperity of the nation depends, form the roof of the coach and support the Crown, resting on a cushion with the Sceptre and Sword of State. The activities are Commerce, with mace and lion, symbolizing domination over the soil, Labor, with hammer and salamander, the personification of fire, Agriculture, with sheaf and sickle, and a sheep representing animal husbandry, and Shipping, with sextant and dolphin.

At the four corners of the roof are miniature figures of children wreathing the Royal Arms with laurel, while cherubim plait triumphal wreaths round the Royal initials above the doors. The cornice bears the coats of arms of the eleven provinces, and in front, larger than the others, those of North Holland and of Amsterdam, the proud donor of the coach. There is a frieze under the windows with symbolic figures in relief representing Religion, the Army, Justice, Art, Science, and Labor. There are cornucopias, the figures of court jesters clasping the ivory handles in their tiny hands, there are lilies and roses; there is the figure of Loyalty and a cartouche containing the year 1898. The beautiful upholstery of the coach is equally worthy of description. Fifteen million tiny stitches in petit point forming a damasked pattern of orange blossoms and cherubs on an ivory-colored background were embroidered by the industrious fingers of scores of needle-women.

The cream colored caleche, another vehicle used by the Royal Family of the Netherlands.

The roof lining is divided into sections, which enabled as many women as possible to share in the work. The sections are enclosed in gilded arches converging to a center-piece formed by the initials of the queen surrounded by a laurel crown and illumined by a matt gold sun. The lining of the coach walls is embroidered with the arms of the Provinces and the State, and with the present and former coats of arms of the City of Amsterdam. The carpet has a pattern of tulips, narcissi, and hyacinths, expressing the idea that the path of the young queen shall be strewn with flowers typical of the country.

Everything has been thought out and worked out down to the minutest details. It is a riot of allegorical figures and animals, flowers and colors. Yet what defies description is the overall impression of harmony and repose that prevails, despite the profuse decoration. The elegant lines, the uniform golden background, the delicate colors and light paintwork all contribute to the harmony and unity which make the Golden Coach the work of art it undoubtedly is.

Such was the plan and such its realization. Then the Presentation Committee was faced with a dilemma. The queen had stated emphatically that she would not accept any presents on the occasion of her inauguration. Not a single exception could be made, not even for a golden coach. The Committee and her Majesty's private secretary exchanged many letters and telegrams and they had many discussions on the subject. Deeply moved by the generosity of the capital, the queen finally decided to accept the gift, not during the inauguration celebrations but at a later date. The young queen must have been delighted with her fairy coach, for the day after her inauguration, September 7th, was fixed for the official presentation, which was duly performed with great ceremony. Since then the Golden Coach has become a familiar sight to all Dutchmen. With few exceptions, it has conveyed the Queen every third Tuesday in September to the historic Hall of Knights to open the new Session of Parliament. On that day, which is popularly called "Princes' Day," people flock to The Hague from far and wide to witness the colorful pageant. The Coach has also added lustre to other celebrations, such as the two occasions on which it carried a radiant young bride to the altar; Queen Wilhelmina in 1901, and Princess Juliana in 1937. Twice, too, the people of the Netherlands have lined the streets along which the Coach has gently borne a royal child, first Princess Juliana and later her eldest daughter, Princess Beatrix, to the baptismal font. It has not carried only youth; on the fiftieth anniversary of the day on which Queen Emma became a citizen of the Netherlands, she drove amidst crowds cheering to express the affection they felt for the Queen Mother of their Country. And it was of course in the Golden Coach that Queen Wilhelmina made her entry into Amsterdam during the celebration of her Silver Jubilee. Amster-

The Golden Coach.

127

dam was also the scene of the ceremonial procession held on the occasion of Queen Juliana's inauguration on September 6, 1948, when, again in the Golden Coach, she drove through the streets with her husband and two older daughters at her side.

Though the Coach has witnessed many joyful events, there have also been darker years, when the country was invaded and occupied by the enemy and the Royal Family was forced to flee. For five years it stood, unused and forgotten, in the Royal Stables where it was found again, miraculously undamaged, in 1945.

Though the Coach was not used in the first few years after the liberation because of the austerity which the Royal Family wished to observe in view of the devastated condition of the country, it has now been fully restored to its former glory.

"Farewell to the Farm"

The coach is at the door at last;
The eager children, mounting fast
And kissing hands, in chorus sing:
Good-bye, good-bye, to everything!

To house and garden, field and lawn,
The meadow-gates we swang upon,
To pump and stable, tree and swing,
Good-bye, good-bye, to everything!

And fare you well for evermore,
O ladder at the hayloft door,
O hayloft where the cobwebs cling,
Good-bye, good-bye, to everything!

Crack goes the whip, and off we go;
The trees and houses smaller grow;
Last, round the woody turn we swing:
Good-bye, good-bye, to everything!

Robert Louis Stevenson

Index